MW00648922

ASSESSMENT LITERACY

Also from the Authors

Literacy in the Disciplines:
A Teacher's Guide for Grades 5–12
Thomas DeVere Wolsey and Diane Lapp

Reading Success for Struggling Adolescent Learners
Edited by Susan Lenski and Jill Lewis

Transforming Writing Instruction in the Digital Age:
Techniques for Grades 5–12
Thomas DeVere Wolsey and Dana L. Grisham

Writing Instruction and Assessment
for English Language Learners K–8
Susan Lenski and Frances Verbruggen

ASSESSMENT LITERACY

AN EDUCATOR'S GUIDE TO UNDERSTANDING ASSESSMENT, K–12

Thomas DeVere Wolsey
Susan Lenski
Dana L. Grisham

Foreword by Diane Lapp

THE GUILFORD PRESS
New York   London

Copyright © 2020 The Guilford Press
A Division of Guilford Publications, Inc.
370 Seventh Avenue, Suite 1200, New York, NY 10001
www.guilford.com

All rights reserved

Except as noted, no part of this book may be reproduced, translated, stored in a retrieval
system, or transmitted, in any form or by any means, electronic, mechanical, photocopying,
microfilming, recording, or otherwise, without written permission from the publisher.

Printed in the United States of America

This book is printed on acid-free paper.

Last digit is print number: 9   8   7   6   5   4   3   2   1

LIMITED DUPLICATION LICENSE

These materials are intended for use only by qualified professionals.

The publisher grants to individual purchasers of this book nonassignable permission to
reproduce all materials for which photocopying permission is specifically granted in a
footnote. This license is limited to you, the individual purchaser, for personal use or use with
your students. This license does not grant the right to reproduce these materials for resale,
redistribution, electronic display, or any other purposes (including but not limited to books,
pamphlets, articles, video- or audiotapes, blogs, file-sharing sites, Internet or intranet sites,
and handouts or slides for lectures, workshops, or webinars, whether or not a fee is charged).
Permission to reproduce these materials for these and any other purposes must be obtained in
writing from the Permissions Department of Guilford Publications.

Library of Congress Cataloging-in-Publication Data is available from the publisher.

ISBN 978-1-4625-4207-9 (paperback)
ISBN 978-1-4625-4208-6 (hardcover)

*In our careers in education, we have had the opportunity
to work with many amazing teachers, professors, and students
at all levels. You will hear many of their voices in this book.*

*In April 2019, one of those colleagues passed away—Dr. Alan N. Crawford,
Professor Emeritus at California State University, Los Angeles.
Alan's work spanned countries from Kazakhstan to Guatemala,
and many more, but he never forgot the students he taught
in the schools of Los Angeles. His work lives on
in the students and friends whose lives he touched.*

*We dedicate this book to Alan and to his belief
that students want to learn and that literacy changes lives.*

About the Authors

Thomas DeVere Wolsey, EdD, teaches graduate courses in research, assessment, and literacy at the American University in Cairo, Egypt, and also leads professional development for teachers throughout the United States and internationally. Previously he taught English and social studies in public schools for 20 years. Dr. Wolsey is the founder of a consulting firm, the Institute to Advance International Education, and has developed training materials for the California Department of Education, TextProject, San Diego State University, and other institutions. His research explores how language informs thinking about content and how the interactions of students in digital and face-to-face environments change their learning. Dr. Wolsey is also interested in the intersections of traditional literacies with digital literacies, focusing specifically on how those literacies affect teacher preparation and professional development.

Dana L. Grisham, PhD, is Professor (retired) at the California State University and is noted for her research on teaching, particularly concerning the intersection of literacy and technology. She has over 80 publications, including books, book chapters, and articles in national and international journals. Dr. Grisham is a past editor of *Reading and Writing Quarterly, Reading Online*, and *The California Reader*.

Susan Lenski, EdD, is Professor of Curriculum and Instruction at Portland State University and a former classroom teacher with 20 years of experience in kindergarten through high school. A member of the Illinois Reading Hall of Fame and a past member of the Board of Directors of the International Literacy Association, Dr. Lenski currently teaches graduate courses and conducts research on strategic reading and writing, adolescent literacy, preparing teacher candidates, and social justice education. She has published more than 65 articles and 14 books.

Foreword

An encyclopedia of information,
A dictionary of terms,
A teacher's guide to instructional examples,
A compilation of ideas for classroom management,
A handbook of research and practice examples.

These are some of the treasures you will find as you read *Assessment Literacy: An Educator's Guide to Understanding Assessment, K–12*. Really, can one book share this much information, while maintaining our interest as readers? Yes, this book does. Can one book really present each of these components fully and well? Yes, this book does. Can one book be your reference guide to multiple types of assessment? Yes, this book can. Will one book be your "go to" every time you want to know something about designing assessments that promote your instruction and your students' learning? Yes, *Assessment Literacy: An Educator's Guide to Understanding Assessment, K–12*, is simply the most useful book I have read about assessment.

I know I am promising you a lot, so let me show you exactly how these authors have shared all of this valuable content inside one book.

While it is chock-full of information to help you understand the various types of assessment, the book supports you in understanding how to design and use these various assessments, the reasons for doing so, and how to use the resulting data to plan the next steps of instruction to promote student learning. It doesn't stop here. The authors then show you how to share data with students, with the goal of enabling them to become self-actualized learners who are able to assess their own learning.

After you read this book, you might find that having a *positive* view of assessment is a welcome change. So often the topic of assessment elicits groans because it reminds us of tests and failures. Probably each of us has received a grade that was below our expectations for our performance. Too often the poor grade has not been accompanied by next-step growth suggestions or even details about why we didn't succeed. Here's my own assessment horror story.

I remember once when I received a D– on an essay that I had brilliantly titled "An Analytical Investigation of Hamlet's Sanity." It was one of my very early attempts at reading Shakespeare, and in addition to grappling with the language, I definitely was grappling with the concepts. How was I to realize that Hamlet's "insanity" was tied directly to his familial struggles? Of course, who wouldn't be somewhat insane if his dead dad appeared as a ghost and asked him to kill his murderer—an uncle? However, at 19, this unsolved mystery was not included in my analysis. I still have this essay, even though I wrote it as a freshman in college.

My teacher put a big red D– on the paper, with the words "You missed the point." I must say it took me years to reread or see the play, and it certainly dented my beliefs in myself as a critical analyst and a lover of Shakespeare. Even sharing the experience still hurts, because I had willingly taken on the task of the assignment, which was to read and analyze a play. I was on my own. There had been no coaching along the way, no conferring about my topic selection, no pointers on how to get started, no suggestions regarding key features to consider when writing an analytical review, and certainly no response-to-intervention scaffolds for revision or allowance that this might be a first draft. There were no formative suggestions or concluding revise-and-resubmit options. I worked independently on this assignment from start to finish. I was in college, and I learned through this assignment that no gradual release of responsibility existed in this course. I also learned another huge lesson from this experience: never to play out this scenario as a teacher.

I have since learned, as a teacher, that there must be a purpose for assessment that aligns closely with the instructional plan and a process to ensure that the resulting assessment data continually influence subsequent learning and instruction. My colleagues Thomas DeVere Wolsey, Susan Lenski, and Dana L. Grisham share this so well in Chapter 1. They note that teachers need to know their students, know how to match them with the lesson purpose, and know how to design instruction that is revised and managed through assessment data that support learning. Chapters 2–4 provide assessment models and examples that highlight the importance of identifying *what* to assess and *how* to do it in ways that will promote student learning during whole-class and small-group instruction. Chapter 5 introduces various types of assessment tools and the practical considerations for using each type. Chapters 6 and 7 teach us the value of self-evaluating our own performance as educators, thereby ensuring that our students gain the insights they need to develop the skills that advance their knowledge and performance. Finally, Chapters 8 and 9 prepare you to share all that you have learned about assessment with your colleagues as you refine your own assessment-based practice.

As you read these chapters, you'll really come to understand why observing your students' natural behaviors as they read, converse, and write across the disciplines will support your initial instructional planning and subsequent modifications, which should be based on your students' performances. Student assessment provides you with the data you need to differentiate instruction. You may be thinking, "Of course I want to differentiate, but how is this really possible when I teach so many students? How can I really manage all of this?" The instructional scenarios in this book offer glimpses into teacher–student communications that show you it is possible to provide very individualized next-step instruction to each student because you are present in their learning growth.

There is much to learn about instructional practice from reading this book. I hope that when you finish, you'll also have new questions about assessment, learning progressions, planning, instruction, and grouping configurations. These are the areas we must continually study and question if we are going to make positive learning differences for each of our students, and also for ourselves as educators.

Enjoy your reading and your professional development!

DIANE LAPP, EdD
Distinguished Professor of Education, San Diego State University;
Instructional coach and teacher, Health Sciences High and Middle College

Contents

Contents

Purchasers of this book can download and print
enlarged versions of the reproducible figures
and appendices at *www.guilford.com/wolsey3-forms*
for personal use or use with their students
(see copyright page for details).

CHAPTER 1

Assessment Tells a Story

Your favorite story, told through cinema, through a short story, through a novel, or around a campfire, is a distillation of the most relevant bits of information, experience, and culture. Why do the stories of Indiana Jones and the starship *Enterprise* endure? Because each tells a story that we recognize, but in a way we hadn't thought of before. What if the assessments used in our classrooms and our schools to inform our state policies were explained in a way that helps teachers, principals, legislators, and especially our students weave a story that is memorable for everyone? In this book, we are going to show you how. The story is just beginning.

Recently, one of the authors (Thomas) visited a classroom in a remote region of a country in Central America. There, I found teachers who loved to teach and students who were engaged in their learning in almost every classroom. A new math teacher was struggling, though. He is an expert mathematician with a great deal of experience in business, but teaching was new to him. When my colleagues and I visited his classroom, we found students whose math skills ran the spectrum from learning how to do three-column addition to students who could do long division with ease. The teacher was following the curriculum, even with fidelity, but he did not know what his students could do or where they might be struggling. We introduced a simple diagnostic instrument to help him learn how to address students' particular needs through grouping, individual guided work, and whole-class instruction.

One young man, on seeing the long-division problem we wrote on the board, actually pumped his fist and smiled excitedly because he knew how to do the math. He was stymied and bored by having to do the addition work he already knew so well. Imagine, being excited about long division! I wished I had my camera to capture that moment. What the math teacher needed was useful information about what his students knew and could do before he began his instruction.

Of course, the purpose of this story is to highlight the value of effective assessment techniques. Many teachers around the world struggle as they try to understand what their students know and can do and then make the fine adjustments those students need. This book is written to help teachers refine their approach to assessment.

Teachers in the 21st century have access to more data than teachers at any other time in history. Data about the students they teach, the classes they lead, and the schools and school systems in which they teach represent mountains of information, much of it available with a couple of clicks of the mouse. However, data and information are one thing; knowledge and wisdom are another. How does a teacher manage the information available and turn it into the sort of wisdom for which teachers are rightly famous?

Teachers are often viewed as persons who know a great deal, but a secret most teachers keep is that they are actually magicians who help others know for themselves. *Assessment literacy* is about the magic of knowing what knowledge and skills they need to engage their students as they learn. It is about the magic of making assessment knowledge useful to students and more than just a score on a test. It is about helping parents and policymakers transform assessment information into wisdom that serves the students for whom they care.

THE PURPOSE AND VALUE OF ASSESSMENT IN EDUCATION

According to O'Connor (2018), there are four main purposes for assessment:

1. Instructional uses—to clarify learning goals, to indicate students' strengths and weaknesses, to demonstrate students' personal–social development, and to contribute to student motivation.
2. Communicative uses—to inform parents or guardians about the learning program of the school and how well their children are achieving the intended learning goals.
3. Administrative uses—to determine promotion and graduation, award honors, determine athletic eligibility, and report to other schools and prospective employers (Gronlund & Linn, 1990).
4. Guidance uses—to help students make their educational and vocational plans realistically.

The area of assessment literacy has been studied and discussed for nearly three decades (Stiggins, 2005), but as assessment instruments evolve with technology and public perceptions of education change, we assert that teachers need a reliable guide to staying current. Recognizing the value of assessment and how it functions in the school and in the wider world are an important part of what it means to be a teacher today (Popham, 2009).

A first step toward improving student educational outcomes is to assist teachers in knowing what their own skills are relative to assessment (e.g., Howell, 2013), and then chart a course to learn and use appropriate assessments that inform engaging and effective instruction.

Assessing difficult-to-measure skills is a challenge. Teachers of science, for example, have long known that students harbor misconceptions about the nature of the world (e.g., a genetic marker for tallness may be viewed as more "powerful" than a marker for being short). To correct students' misunderstandings, it is important for educators to know how to ask themselves questions about what students do and do not understand, and then to act in the classroom on the basis of that knowledge (e.g., Gottheiner & Seigel, 2012). The same may be said about guiding students' future growth.

Literacy learning presents particular challenges to educators because language learning crosses all content areas and domains. It addresses learning that is difficult to grasp, such as the critical thinking problem the science teacher just described might face, and reading comprehension skills, such as determining the theme of a work of literature where there is no single correct answer. Writing, similarly, is challenging to assess and is even more difficult to evaluate when teachers need to make decisions based on the whole classroom.

Most important, perhaps, all the assessment information that schools collect is of no value unless teachers put that information to use day by day in the classroom in planning instruction and in communicating with others. Checking for understanding (Hunter, 1982) and providing useful and respectful feedback (e.g., Wolsey, 2008) are the necessary next steps.

WHAT ASSESSMENTS DO

Assessment implies gathering useful information and making decisions based on that information. Take a minute to get a piece of paper and pen, or open a word processing document on your computer or mobile phone. Set a timer for 5 minutes and list all the types of assessments you make as a teacher in a given day. We will be right here when you return.

[*Five minutes later.*]

Okay. That list is fairly long, right? Each day you have to decide whether Sara needs to go see the nurse, what Fredrico needs to do to make up for an absence, and whether John really does understand that difficult science concept. That's just the beginning. Other decisions include how much time to allow students to work on an assignment, whether to have students read in small groups or silently, and when to order supplies for next week's activity. What is the best way to explain to Crystal's parents those high-stakes test scores? What is the best way for students to demonstrate that they really do understand the theme of that novel?

Every teacher knows well how many decisions must be made to nudge students toward improvement and engagement with learning. On that same piece of paper with your list, state whether you agree or not with each of these statements. Use the scale of "strongly disagree," "disagree," "not sure," "agree," and "strongly agree." Ready?

- *Assessment and evaluation mean approximately the same thing.*
- *How students score on high-stakes assessments is a fairly good indicator of the quality of the teacher's skills.*
- *Because high-stakes tests cover a lot of ground, it is the teacher's job to cover it all.*
- *Assessments are objective.*
- *Assessments are subjective.*
- *I would really rather just teach and not worry about assessment.*

Let's take a look at each one of these statements.

Assessment and evaluation mean approximately the same thing.

This myth is an easy one to dispel because so often the terms are used interchangeably by people who are *not* educators. For those of us who must regularly assess and evaluate the students in our care, the difference is subtle but extremely important.

According to Merriam-Webster, an *assessment* is "the action or an instance of making a judgment about something." An *evaluation,* on the other hand, requires affixing value to a condition, or "to determine the significance, worth, or condition of usually by careful appraisal and study."[1]

The definitions may seem similar, but making a judgment about something, in this case student learning, is worlds apart from determining the significance or worth of that learning. For example, you might notice that your students have misunderstood the phrase "lightning never strikes in the same place twice" by somehow imbuing that electricity-charged bolt of energy from the sky with intentions (e.g., "I've been here; I'll strike somewhere else"). But you don't have to assign *value* to that assessment. The only action you need to take, as a teacher, is to find a way to change the misconception.

Both assessment and evaluation involve taking action of some type; however, assigning value to what is assessed is a very different thing. We think that in helping students, parents, administrators, and policymakers shape a useful story, choosing what value to assign and what actions to take are of critical importance.

We know already that assessment is a process whereby teachers gather information about their students, their school, and many other factors dependent on the

---

[1] For *assessment: www.merriam-webster.com/dictionary/assessment*; for *evaluate: www. merriam-webster.com/ dictionary/evaluate.*

context of teaching (e.g., the community). Then, once they have that information, they must make a decision of some type. Isn't that the same as evaluation? Let's turn to the dictionary again.

Dictionary.com defines *evaluate* this way:

1. to determine or set the value or amount of; appraise: *to evaluate property.*
2. to judge or determine the significance, worth, or quality of; assess: *to evaluate the results of an experiment.*
3. *Mathematics.* to determine or calculate the numerical value of (a formula, function, relation, etc.).[2]

Whereas assessment suggests following a path or making a decision on the basis of information gathered, evaluation focuses on assigning a value or determining the worth of something. In this sense, evaluation is one way to make an assessment because a decision has been made to assign a value to a performance, product, or behavior. On the other hand, assessment involves many other types of decisions. We think of evaluation as a subset of assessment. Put another way, all evaluations are types of assessments, but not all assessments result in evaluation.

Coming to Terms

Evaluation and assessment are common terms in teaching with overlapping and complementary meanings. They are also used interchangeably, at times, so clarifications are in order about how this book employs the terms. Evaluation is a static event—the test at the end of the unit, the culminating project with attendant rubrics, the final score, and the final grade. But we need to remind ourselves that there is a danger in thinking that a grade or score is the same thing as proof of learning. Linguist Alfred Korzybski pointed out the logical problem of mistaking a map or other representation for the thing itself; he explained, "A map is not the territory" (1933, p. 750). Evaluative instruments are a kind of map, and learning is the territory for schools today. Put simply, a low score on a test does not necessarily mean a student learned nothing, and stagnant aggregate scores for a school do not mean good instruction and important learning do not occur there.

Assessment, as we use the term in this book, has a different meaning. Of course, assessment and evaluation are related concepts and can go on simultaneously. Consider the origin of the word *assess*. It derives from the Latin *assidēre*, which in turn comes from the word for "sit." One who assesses sits beside a judge to help. Of course, it helps to set aside the historical reason an assistant was sitting next to the judge: the assistant's job was to assess the taxes on a property or levy a fine. The point is, assessment is dynamic and an integral part of formulating our own judgments about instruction and learning.

---

[2] *www.dictionary.com/browse/evaluate.*

Complicating how we understand the terms evaluation and assessment are the related terms *formative assessment* and *summative assessment*. We might define formative assessment as collecting and interpreting information about *ongoing learning* that can be used to improve both instruction and learning. The dynamic and interactive nature of formative assessment catches students and teachers at work and in action (Hagstrom, 2006), adjusting the course of the learning process as they go. It is nuanced and often precise. Summative assessment is more closely associated with the definition provided earlier for evaluation—a static event in an instructional cycle. Summative assessment tends to cast a long shadow, and it gives the appearance of both objectivity and finality. The shadow obscures other forms of useful assessments that move learning and learners forward.

Consider the first-grade student who makes many miscues while reading aloud. The teacher makes an assessment about the type of miscues made and adjusts instruction accordingly. Grades are not assigned to such an assessment (though there are scores that guide decision making) because the aim of the assessment is to help the child improve as a reader.

> ### How students score on high-stakes assessments is a fairly good indicator of the quality of the teacher's skills.

National Board Certified teachers reported in a study (Vandevoort, Amrein-Beardsley, & Berliner, 2004) that they did not believe that high-stakes tests (in this case, the Stanford Achievement Test, 9th edition, or SAT-9) were a reliable assessment of everything they did in the classroom. Many claimed that they purposefully did not attempt to teach their students to succeed on the exam. Doing so was not why they chose to teach.

National Board Certified teachers undergo a rigorous process to achieve certification that demonstrates mastery of these five core propositions:

Proposition 1. Teachers are committed to students and their learning.
Proposition 2. Teachers know the subjects they teach and how to teach those subjects to students.
Proposition 3. Teachers are responsible for managing and monitoring student learning.
Proposition 4. Teachers think systematically about their practice and learn from experience.
Proposition 5. Teachers are members of learning communities.[3]

However, Vandervoort and colleagues (2004) found that students taught by National Board Certified teachers tend to achieve at a higher rate than those

---

[3] Retrieved from *www.nbpts.org/standards-five-core-propositions*.

taught by non–Board Certified teachers. One way to describe the analysis is that it seemed that Board Certified teachers were able to achieve 1.2 more months' worth of instruction, as indicated by the SAT-9, than their noncertified peers, or about 25 more days' worth of teaching than noncertified teachers. Wow.

Even though the study's authors were able to predict the achievement of Board Certified teachers, it does not stand to reason that teachers should be evaluated on the basis of any single indicator, such as the SAT-9. Many factors are beyond the direct control of the school and of teachers. A family's socioeconomic status, parental level of education, quality of nutrition, and even how much sleep a child gets all play a role in achievement in school. While we don't agree that teachers are defined by their students' test scores, we can agree that effective teachers do all they can to overcome challenges, even those they don't directly control.

> **WHAT IS A HIGH-STAKES TEST?**
>
> *High-stakes tests* come in many different types. They typically carry heavy rewards or consequences to the test taker, the teacher, the school, and sometimes an entire nation. For example, the California High School Exit Exam (CAHSEE; California Department of Education, 2018) was used between 2006 and 2016, and students were required to pass the exam in order to receive a high school diploma. Because the test carried substantial consequences and students' diplomas were on the line, we can consider it a high-stakes test. Any test, no matter the type, that is used to make important decisions or to hold a student, teacher, school, or other stakeholder accountable can be considered high stakes.

Because high-stakes tests cover a lot of ground, it is the teacher's job to cover it all.

Teaching all students to be prepared for high-stakes tests may seem like a daunting task, and that's because it is. But it's not impossible if the exams do what they say they do. For example, Partnership for Assessment of Readiness for College and Careers (PARCC)—a mouthful to be sure—claims that their tests are accurate measures:

> PARCC is computer-based and uses interactive questions to determine whether students have mastered the fundamentals, as well as higher-order skills such as critical thinking, problem-solving, and analyzing sources to write arguments and informational essays—skills not easily assessed by traditional multiple-choice tests. (PARCC, 2017, *Why PARCC?*, para. 2)

If the authors of PARCC are right, then maybe the test is still a challenge, but an attainable one. Don't we teach problem-solving skills and critical thinking anyway? If so, the content on the exam is only relevant to the extent that students can make sense of it in order to solve a problem or analyze sources, and so on. We revisit this idea later in this book.

Assessments are objective.

Experts in educational assessment often use a fairly easy-to-understand definition of what an objective assessment is: one whose measurement derives from questions or prompts that have one, and only one, unique answer. If this isn't what you thought we were going to propose, well, keep reading!

Assessments are subjective.

All right, if objective assessment questions have only one correct answer, then subjective assessments must be the kind that have many possible correct answers. If that's what you are thinking, you are right. But doesn't that avoid the problem of determining what is correct and what is not? Just how objective can humans be about complex thinking, such as writing arguments or sussing out the theme of a novel? What if a teacher's expected response is subjective in such a way that students can't discern what they are supposed to learn or adjust how they learn? Good questions. Chapter 4 goes into these interesting issues in greater detail.

I would really rather just teach and not worry about assessment.

In an educational landscape where benchmark tests, placement tests, standardized tests, and other tests dominate our classrooms, escape from the world of assessment would seem a dream come true. Early in this chapter, we suggested that assessment can be part of the arc of a student's (or a school's) story. Good stories, the ones worth remembering, are those that are woven from carefully selected yarns. Selecting the right yarns for our tale is the secret.

But, seriously, what about the evaluations from *others?*

The publishers of various assessment instruments want educators to believe that their particular evaluation service or instrument is just what you need to be a successful teacher. The school principal likely uses some type of tool to evaluate teachers, and that tool seems important in different ways as well. Our students know that the test at the end of the unit will boost or deflate their grades. And parents care about grades, of course.

Pearson Education promotes the *Developmental Reading Assessment®, 2nd Edition Plus,* app this way:

> Incorporating the DRA2+ App eliminates multiple tasks in the administration of individual student reading proficiency. Teachers simply logon their tablet, set up the assessment for each student, then assess their reading session while the student is reading the passage.[4]

---

[4]Retrieved from *www.pearsonassessments.com/products/100001222/developmental-reading-assessment-2nd-edition-plus-dra2-dra2.html#tab-details.*

What could be easier, right? Another popular reading assessment suggests:

The University of Oregon's Center on Teaching and Learning (UO CTL) is the home of DIBELS® 8th Edition, the best-available tool for assessing the efficacy of literacy instruction and programs. DIBELS 8th Edition is the way to know if your literacy instruction and programs work.[5]

What teacher wouldn't want the best available tool? We are not suggesting that these instruments are or are not useful, but we are hinting that teachers are best suited to choose the appropriate instruments, determine which ones serve the interests of their students, and interpret the information from their own classroom-based assessments and those published by others. In the next chapters, we explore together how that might be done and how teachers can help students, parents, administrators, and themselves, of course, to weave together a story worth telling.

TELLING A STORY WITH ASSESSMENT

Throughout this book, we make use of story archetypes to provide tips and traps (challenges) to our readers. *Archetypes* are foundational character patterns that are recognizable across cultures and languages (Truby, 2007). Here are the story archetypes we chose:

- *The wise teacher.* Wise teachers include Yoda from *Star Wars* and Polonius in *Hamlet*. The wise teacher provides guidance for other characters that will help them live a better life. They can be too set in their ways, at times, making their strength a potential weakness.
- *The professor.* A variation on the wise teacher. We use the professor archetype when we can share our work with teachers and students around the globe. The professor is sometimes a teacher, sometimes a magician, a trickster now and then, and a rebel on occasion.
- *The magician.* Magicians are able to help others see beyond the obvious. A magician gone bad can potentially use her or his skills to disrupt instead of to bring order. Merlin in the King Arthur tales is a magician, and of course most of the characters in the Harry Potter series share this archetype. Magician tips in this book highlight technology for assessment.
- *The trickster.* Tricksters are popular because they advance the story action through confidence games and trickery. Batman's Joker is a trickster, as is Br'er Rabbit. The tricksters in our story of assessment show us where assessment traps may lie.

---

[5] Retrieved from *https://dibels.uoregon.edu/assessment/dibels/dibels-eighth-edition*.

- ***The sage leader, or royalty.*** Like King Arthur, the goddess Hera, or the Skipper in *Gilligan's Island,* the authority figure or king and queen archetypes provide leadership, wisdom, and protection. Occasionally they let power get the better of them, but in our story, the authorities foster growth. Throughout this book, we use the royalty archetype to provide tips that effective principals and other school administrators use. We hope the term *royalty* does not go to their heads!

- ***The rebel.*** Rebels stand out and don't mind taking a position that is counter to the crowd. Sometimes in teaching, we encounter situations or contexts that are just accepted at face value. The rebel pushes back against these tendencies. Han Solo, Holden Caulfield, and Achilles exemplify the rebel archetype.

- ***The hero.*** The hero of our story is you, dear reader, and so are your students. The hero of our tale is also a wise teacher. As you can see, characters can be more than one archetype. Let's tell a story.

In several places throughout this book, we provide *assessments of the assessments* we are discussing. Our purpose is to offer checkpoints or benchmarks you can use to monitor your own use of assessments. There are four *Assessing the Assessments* forms:

- Assessing the Assessments: Gathering Information and Evidence (Figure 2.2, Chapter 2)
- Assessing the Assessments: Interpreting and Analyzing Assessment Data (Figure 2.4, Chapter 2)
- Assessing the Assessments: Quality (Chapter 6)
- Assessing the Assessments: Documenting and Record Keeping (Chapter 8)

You can find blank templates for these assessment forms in Appendices A–D, or download them from this book's website (see the box at the end of the table of contents). We have also included these assessments at places in the text that we believe are most relevant, but these tools are useful for many topics in this book.

CHAPTER 2

How Do I Know What to Assess?

Teachers make decisions constantly, both planned and unplanned. A widely used figure suggests that teachers make around 1,500 decisions every day. Read up on this if you are curious.[1] Researchers at Carnegie Mellon and Temple universities (Koedinger, Booth, & Klahr, 2013) suggest that teachers make decisions based on the type of learning required by the students. Is Ahmed's understanding of the material the same as Beth's? If not, what instructional technique is likely to be most effective for each student? When should feedback be provided? Should it be given immediately, or after the student has time to think through the processes of completing the assigned task? Is the instructional approach for relatively simple learning the same as for more complex or abstract learning? You can probably surmise that most teachers could expand this list of possible decisions infinitely. Okay, maybe we exaggerate—or maybe not. Koedinger and colleagues (2013) identified several instructional techniques and different dosage levels (e.g., the spacing in time of similar learning tasks) and came up with the following astounding calculation reported in the prestigious journal *Science*.

> If we consider just 15 of the 30 instructional techniques we identified, three alternative, dosage levels, and the possibility of different dosage choices for early and late instruction, we compute 3^{15*2} or 205 trillion options. (p. 935)

Wow! At the same time, students also have choices to make. Do I begin this essay with an anecdote, or should I jump right into the topic? Am I reading this essay to gain information, to enjoy the material, or some combination of both (e.g.,

---

[1] Larry Cuban's thoughts on teacher decision making are here: *https://larrycuban.wordpress.com/2011/06/16/jazz-basketball-and-teacher-decision-making*; Larry Ferlazzo shares his ideas here: *http://larryferlazzo.edublogs.org/2014/02/22/quote-of-the-day-have-you-ever-wondered-how-many-decisions-we-teachers-need-to-make-each-day.*

Rosenblatt, 1995)? I'm having trouble understanding this text, so is it worth it to stop and try to summarize it?

Every time a decision is made by students and by their teachers, there is an opportunity for assessment. Not every one of these intersections of decisions by students and teachers warrants assessment, of course. But we educators are left with a host of questions. What student behaviors and products deserve our attention? Which of our own teaching behaviors and experiences should we self-assess? And, most important, what do we do with the assessment data and insights gathered?

ASSESSMENT THAT TELLS A STORY: HOW MUCH IS JUST RIGHT?

Stories often involve a problem and a resolution, whether that resolution is good, bad, unexpected, or something else. Consider poor Hamlet. Is he ready to be king? Does he want to be? What about his moral code that presents a difficulty when his ghost father suggests he murder Claudius? If ever there was a problem, this might be it: "Dad wants me to murder his murderer; should I?"

Hamlet's problem is probably not something you will face in your classroom, but the idea of determining how and what we teach and learn is important. By problematizing teaching and learning, we must think about the best ways forward or the best course corrections when necessary. One other point about the stories assessments can help tell is that these stories are always coauthored by the students with our help and guidance.

KNOWING OUR STUDENTS

Because our assessment stories should have satisfactory and happy endings, unlike poor Hamlet, our first stop on the road to telling that story is to know our students. For most teachers we have met, this goes without saying. They know their students' interests; their readiness to learn a skill, strategy, or concept; their eagerness to tell what happened in the lunchroom or what happened at home last week when a favorite uncle passed away; and much more. But knowing our students has particular implications for assessment as well.

A student's first language, if not the language of the school, is a prime consideration for teachers and how they assess student learning. The same can be said of cultural or ethnic differences. Students who cannot read a test question because it is in a language they have not yet mastered are at a disadvantage no matter how much they know about the subject or skill to be learned.

How do teachers get to know their students? If you are reading this book, you likely are a teacher or work with teachers closely, and you could easily write this section yourself. Still, it's worth taking a little time to review what teachers do that helps them to know and understand their students.

Cumulative Files

This is going in your permanent record. Did anyone tell you that when you were in school, whether for an accomplishment or as a kind of warning? Permanent records or *cumulative files* (cums) can be useful, but it is paramount to remember that these files are legal or regulatory documents, not a picture of who a student is or what she can be. We agree with the sentiment expressed by teachers who say they do not look through cum files at the beginning of the year to get a sense of who the students are because starting with predetermined notions of what students are capable of achieving is problematic if our business is to guide students to productive time in our classrooms.

With the advent of increasingly sophisticated student information systems (SIS), vast amounts of data are available to teachers, ready to be punched up on a laptop on demand. Cum files in the digital age contain testing data, information about home languages spoken, behavior records, and much more. This information can be overwhelming, creating what John McCarthy (2014) of the website *Edutopia* calls "assessment fog." In an assessment fog, so much information is available that it can obscure the path forward and lead teachers and students alike into a thicket.

The cum file can be useful beyond its purpose as a legal document. A student who needs particular attention can benefit when his teacher examines the information in the file looking for patterns in attendance, grades, behaviors, and high-stakes test scores. The secret is to open the file for the purpose of helping a student succeed, never to prejudge or pigeonhole a student into categories in our minds that become self-fulfilling prophecies for the student. Rather, look for strengths, interests, and struggles the student faces that you can use as a foundation for a successful future and happy ending to the story.

Stand at the Door

When I (Thomas) taught middle school students, I made a practice of greeting them at the classroom door, nearly every day and every period. Why? First, I learned their names very quickly. The students quickly learned the rules, too. If I missed some as a large group came through the door, they called me out. "Hey, you didn't say 'hi' to me!" And, of course, I then did so. The practice had benefits for classroom discipline as well. Students who had a rough time at home or on the playground were met with a smile. It is hard to stay upset when someone just said "hi" and was happy to see you.

Each day, students came through the door and told me about a new baby sister, a sick brother, or an award from the chorus class, and that made it possible for me to respond, "How is that new baby sister?"; "Did you win your football game last night?" These things matter, and little by little, students can come to trust the teacher who puts aside all the administrative stuff (catching up on attendance, filling out the lunch count form) at the beginning of class and meets them at the door. Little by little, the teacher begins to know each and every student who is pursuing a learning adventure that day.

Wander Around

The other teachers nicknamed him "Ditto" because he spent his conference or preparation period running off reams of packets that students would silently complete during class. When the bell rang, the students knew to file in, to take a packet, and to work until the bell rang again at the end of class. Out they would file, and a new class filed in as Ditto sat in his chair at the back of the room reading his newspaper. Not a very exciting class, but the students sure knew what to do, and they did it. Until one day. You have likely figured out that this is fiction, from the movie *Teachers* (Levinson, Russo, Russo, & Hiller, 1984). Today, photocopiers have replaced ditto machines, so imagine the teacher who is in a panic because the copy machine is not working on a particular day and you'll have Ditto.

Then, one day, Ditto died while reading the paper. His chair kept him upright, and rigor mortis set in. None of the students noticed, and the bell rang. Out filed the students, and a new group came in, took their packets, and began to work. About halfway through the class, Ditto toppled over in his chair. The students noticed.

Ditto is a caricature, but he serves to make a useful point. Sometimes our desks beckon with grading to do, scores to record, and reports to file with the school administration. Get up anyway. Wander around the room. Look at the work students are doing as they are doing it. Listen to small groups process complex ideas and explain challenging concepts.

 Professor tip: We explore this idea and its relationship to assessment in more detail later. For now, it is also a good way to learn what our students know, what they can do, and what they care about.

Student Conferences

Meeting, however briefly, with our students is a good way to get to know who they are. Doing so can be a challenge in a classroom with 30 or 40 kids in it, but it can be done. Confer with students about their writing with gentle nudges to help them improve. Confer with them about their progress as well as their struggles in class. Confer in order to understand a behavior you find to be a problem. Getting to know students this way builds trust and helps you know more about your students and how best to communicate with them. Quick note: You might have noticed that we used the term *confer* instead of the terms *conference* or *conferencing*. Why? Because the perfectly good English verb *confer* already exists, and it's shorter!

KNOWING STANDARDS AND OBJECTIVES

At the top of most written lesson-plan templates there is a space for standards. Often there is a space for objectives or outcomes as well. This space is always placed at the top before any of the lesson activities are described. It is not just a convenient place to include this information; the space is at the top for a reason. Standards and objectives should drive the types of learning activities that are included in any lesson. Stiggins (2005) used the term *learning targets* to indicate what it is that students should know and be able to do. Some time ago, Grant Wiggins and Jay McTighe (2005) proposed what they called "backward design," in contrast to what they called "forward design," in which teachers choose the activities in which students will engage and the instruction they will provide. In their view, forward design presents a problem because it focuses on what the teacher does and directs students to do. A side effect of this approach is that the activities and instruction can be, and often are, mistaken for learning.

To remedy this, Wiggins and McTighe coined the term *backward design* to suggest that the first part of any lesson (or unit or course) has to be determining what the learning goals, targets, or objectives should be. The second part of lesson planning is determining what an effective performance of the learning target might look like. Only then is it a good idea to move to the third part of backward design—determining which types of instruction and which activities will guide the students to achieve that target.

> **OBJECTIVES, OUTCOMES, AND STANDARDS**
>
> Often these terms are used interchangeably, but they do mean slightly different things. An *objective* is what a teacher plans for her students to learn, and an *outcome* is what students actually learned. Ideally, objectives and outcomes are always the same, so it makes sense that the terms are used the same way. In schools that rely on *standards* (and which schools don't these days?), the standards guide the learning objectives. Standards are not necessarily the same thing as objectives, either. An objective guides students toward mastery of the standard, often in conjunction with other, related objectives.
>
> Objectives are what students should learn at the end of the lesson, however long that lesson might be. Sometimes that learning is accomplished in one class session or period, and other times it extends across several days.

 Wise teacher tip: Knowing what students should be able to do is not the same as asking them to complete an activity or worksheet. Activities do not necessarily equal learning.

A little over 40 years ago, a researcher at the University of California, Los Angeles, noticed something irregular about the basal reading books she found in teachers' classrooms. Irregular, or perhaps downright odd. The teachers' editions of the basal readers prompted teachers to do two things: assign and assess (Durkin, 1981). Durkin (1990) analyzed the texts and discovered that the books had no provision for direct instruction. Her research on reading comprehension instruction revealed that less than 1% of the time spent during reading at school was devoted to comprehension instruction. Most of the classroom time was spent assessing comprehension through the teacher asking questions about what students had been assigned to read. Years later, the RAND Study Group (2002) found that teachers in the primary and upper elementary grades still did not devote adequate time to comprehension instruction.

There are a few lessons we can derive from this example. Relying on supplied materials, such as a basal reader, for instructional guidance may not be the best instructional strategy. The other lesson is that teachers are in the best position to determine what objectives are to be met, what a good performance demonstrating understanding of that objective looks like, and what activities and instruction will most likely lead to that outcome.

Effective assessment rests on knowing what concepts, knowledge, skills, and dispositions students should achieve based on the standards that inform curriculum planning and on having a clear plan, based on objectives, to guide students to success. An extra benefit: If students know and understand what they are attempting to learn and what learning performances look like, they are more likely to be successful.

STORIES FROM THE CLASSROOM

Quentin Fields teaches 11th-grade English Language Arts at James Logan High School in Union City, California. Here he describes how he assessed a problem his students encountered with public speaking and how he used assessment to help them overcome the challenge.

How I Determined My Thesis and Its Effects on Public-Speaking Students

QUENTIN FIELDS

As a first-year teacher, the thought of saving the world one child at a time is what dictates which lessons are prepared. Well, that and the state standards, of course.

It was in my first year that I decided to take a different approach in teaching both argumentative writing and discourse: I created a debate unit. Seeing that I was teaching 11th grade, I figured that giving students an opportunity to practice their argumentative skills in a professional setting would prove to be fun and helpful. Students were organized into teams and therefore had a support system in place to help them when the day came to present their argument against another team. Unfortunately, I began to witness multiple students struggle when tasked with speaking in front of the class. However, it wasn't until one student actually had an anxiety attack that I realized how difficult public speaking could be for students.

Fast forward to the next year, and just before we started the argumentative unit, I held a discussion with each class. We focused on the reasons why students tend to have more anxiety when speaking in front of the class than at any other time. Students began to share many reasons, such as self-consciousness, lack of preparation, and even a lack of interest in the topic. After holding this class conversation, I decided to use this opportunity to focus my master's thesis on how to reduce anxiety among high school students during public speaking.

Our first step was to try different methods before and during the public speaking presentations. Some students presented with the lights off in order to see if a darkened room decreased their feeling of self-consciousness or inadequacy. Others used slide shows to take the focus off them, giving the audience a visual aid to occupy their eyes. In order to allow for better preparation and stimulate interest in the topic, students were allowed to choose anything they wanted to inform their classmates about. We even had students compare sitting and standing during their speeches, and it was interesting to see the difference in the level of comfort displayed between the two presentation styles. Speaking with confidence is half the battle, and after each presentation, the audience provided positive feedback to help generate more confidence for future speaking situations. In a sense, having students present informative speeches before the argumentative debate unit gave them more confidence and an opportunity to share something they truly cared about.

Finally, students were assessed based on a rubric that evaluated the multiple areas involved in public speaking (see Figure 2.1). Students were to try to maintain a proper posture; to feel comfortable with the audience; and to have appropriate volume, speed, and modulation. Last, students were asked to make sure that they were aware of their audience's needs, which is always a challenging task. This required them to try and use relatable examples, jokes, and current events to entice the audience into listening to their speech. In addition to the grading rubric, students also completed a reflection sheet sharing how they felt about their most recent performance compared to past performances. In the end, it was an experience that reminded me of how many factors are part of one's execution when it comes to speaking publicly.

Content	High 5	Mid High 4	Middle 3	Low Mid 2	Low 1
States the purpose.					
Organizes the content.					
Supports ideas.					
Incorporates examples.					
Summarizes the main idea(s).					
Demonstrates awareness of listeners' needs.					
Speaks clearly with appropriate vocabulary and information.					
Uses tone, speed, and volume as tools.					
Posture is straight and still.					
Appears comfortable with audience.					

FIGURE 2.1. Informative speaking rubric.

From *Assessment Literacy: An Educator's Guide to Understanding Assessment, K–12*, by Thomas DeVere Wolsey, Susan Lenski, and Dana L. Grisham. Copyright © 2020 The Guilford Press. Permission to photocopy this figure is granted to purchasers of this book for personal use or use with students (see copyright page for details). Purchasers can download enlarged versions of this figure (see box at the end of the table of contents).

FORMATIVE, SUMMATIVE, AND BENCHMARK ASSESSMENTS

Before we launch into our discussion of what to assess, let's take a brief side trip. Many schemes deconstruct assessment in several useful ways. A quick tour of the approach most familiar to us as teachers should be helpful before we delve into the details of what needs to be assessed and how to do so. The particular instrument or artifact we use for assessment purposes doesn't define whether it is formative or summative. The purpose of the assessment is what counts. We can think of *formative assessments* as guiding learning, *summative assessments* as certifying learning, and *benchmark assessments* as both guiding and tracking learning, according to Kathy Dyer (2017) at NWEA, an educational testing firm based in Oregon.

Formative Assessment

A fairly useful and precise definition of formative assessment is just what we need here. Fortunately, Black and Wiliam (2009) provide one.

> Practice in a classroom is formative to the extent that evidence about student achievement is elicited, interpreted, and used by teachers, learners, or their peers, to make decisions about the next steps in instruction that are likely to be better, or better founded, than the decisions they would have taken in the absence of the evidence that was elicited. (p. 9)

Wiliam (2011) makes clear that formative assessment supports learning rather than determines if learning has occurred. He proposed that formative assessment involves three processes: deciding what the student has currently learned, knowing where she is going, and providing feedback that will help her move forward. These three processes can be acted on by the teacher, by peers, and by the learner herself. Formative assessment is often referred to in practice as "assessment *for* learning," and we use both terms in this book.

Put another way, formative assessment is focused on the student and his progress toward educational objectives. That's important to keep in mind when we turn to a discussion of grading practices and how they fit into our assessment practices. If formative assessment is intended to be useful to the learner, what about summative assessment?

Summative Assessment

Summative assessment is sometimes referred to as "assessment *of* learning," and it emphasizes information that teachers, school administrators, government agencies, educational institutions, and the public may need. Exams at the end of a unit or semester aid the teacher in deciding what was learned and to what degree. High-stakes assessments required by state or federal governments guide policymakers and others as they make educational decisions that affect large populations. Standardized tests for college admission provide information to college admissions officers as they determine which candidates of many would be a good fit for their universities. Summative assessments do not tell us everything about what has been learned, but give us enough to go on, usually after the instruction and learning activities are completed.

To be certain, assessments intended to be summative can be used by teachers to inform future learning events for students or to plan new instruction based on past summative assessment. If you have participated with your teaching colleagues in a professional learning community to analyze last spring's high-stakes test scores and make plans to address areas in need of improvement, you have been using a primarily summative assessment as a formative assessment.

Benchmark Assessments

Somewhere between formative assessments in the classroom and summative assessments at the end of a unit or semester lies the realm of the benchmark or interim assessment. Benchmark assessments often gather data in a way that charts a pattern of growth and makes it possible to predict what instruction is necessary to chart a way forward (see Dyer, 2017). They may also be useful in making appropriate determinations for differentiating instruction as well. Other benchmark assessments use instruments that capture snapshots of learning, such as the third edition of the Fountas and Pinnell Benchmark Assessment System. Earlier we mentioned that benchmarks and interim assessments get a pass on the caveat that the type of assessment is not necessarily determined by the instrument or activity. The reasons are that benchmark assessments are usually designed specifically for that purpose and that they provide formative, summative, and predictive information. With this foundation, we can now turn to the questions of what assessments are needed and how to determine what should be assessed.

GATHERING INFORMATION AND EVIDENCE

For the remainder of this chapter, we focus on formative assessment because it is the assessment form over which teachers have the most control, and which they typically find the most useful. Benchmark and summative assessments are addressed in later chapters. In Chapter 1, we asked you to list a variety of assessments that are routinely part of your classroom practice. These could include observing students' performances; listening in to their groupwork; providing a rubric and models of excellent performances; and exit slips, quizzes, homework assignments, essays, and other written products. Every one of these assessments is a source of useful information about how students are performing and how they might move forward toward achieving objectives and standards.

A little reflective assessment of our own practices might be helpful, so let's give it a try. In Appendix A (see pp. 167–169), you will find an instrument for thinking about a single lesson or instructional event. Across the top of the assessment, there are several instruments or tools that might be used in a formative manner to gather information and evidence about how students are progressing. Along the left side are several types of activities or artifacts of those activities, like those mentioned in the previous paragraph, that students might produce.[2]

In Figure 2.2, we provide an example of how this form might help with the analysis of the many assessment tasks that might occur in your classroom. Not

---

[2]We want to thank Passant Mahmoud at the American University in Cairo for laying the substantial foundation for this instrument and others in this book.

Assessing the Tools

This instrument is designed to analyze and evaluate the different assessment tools used by teachers in class. This assessment serves teachers in terms of "assessment for learning" since it can help them measure the effectiveness of their assessment techniques used throughout the year with their students. Accordingly, they can modify, amend, or change their applied assessment techniques to be able to assess their students more effectively. This is a general assessment tool that is also designed to be applied in many contexts, including different grade levels, different class subjects, different educational systems, and so forth. The criteria in this tool are derived from the assessment steps that teachers originally go through with their students in any educational cycle.

Assessment for Learning Checklist

Standards:

CCSS.ELA-Literacy.W.7.1— Write arguments to support claims with clear reasons and relevant evidence.

Objectives:

Students will be able to identify and analyze the claims made in a written argument.

Students will select and construct claims for an argument paper they will write.

Date: February 4, 2020

Class: 3rd period

Subject: 8th grade English

Teacher: Mr. Yorick

Observer: n/a

(continued)

FIGURE 2.2. Completed example of Appendix A, Assessing the Assessments: *Gathering Information and Evidence.*

21

(C) Content (P) Process (Pr) Product	Assessment Tool	Gathering Information and Evidence						
		Questioning	Observation	Quizzes, Tests, and Exams; Other Work Products	Checklists	Rubrics	Self-Assessment	Peer Assessment
Student Work Products or Activity	**Description**	Teacher asks focused and planned questions to ensure understanding of the material.	Teacher systematically observes and monitors students, including checking for understanding.	Teacher collects written evidence of what the students have learned.	Teacher measures students' learning by matching it to specific criteria in relation to learning outcomes.	Teacher effectively communicates expectations of quality and grading at different levels of achievement.	Teacher allows students to reflect on their own performance, supplying them with defined criteria to measure against.	Teacher allows students to reflect on the performance of their colleagues, supplying them with defined criteria, to measure against.
Homework and Assignments	Teacher assigns students with relevant homework and assignments that further enforce understanding.			*Cornell notes (C) and (P)*		*Rubric (Pr) Written argument (Pr) and (C)*	*Graphic organizer (C) and (P)*	
Informal and Quick Checks Checking for Understanding	Teacher uses exit slips, minute paper, polling with technology.	*Responses to questions— whole class (C)*	*Discussion in pairs or triads (C) and (P)*					

FIGURE 2.2. *(continued)*

Presentations	Teacher allows students to show their learning of the material by presenting it to their classmates.					
Projects	Teacher allows students to deepen and show connection in their learning by working on individual/group projects.					
Behaviors and Dispositions	Teacher promotes behaviors such as collaboration, on-task work, classroom routines, cognitive strategies, and critical thinking.		Goal 18 (P)			
Comments						

FIGURE 2.2. (*continued*)

every instrument, work product, or artifact will appear in every lesson, so don't worry if some boxes are blank.

Imagine an eighth-grade lesson in which students are learning the fine art of argumentation as indicated in the Common Core State Standards (National Governors Association [NGA] & Council of Chief State School Officers [CCSSO], 2010). First the teacher shows a video clip explaining how argumentation is used in everyday life. Next, he introduces a couple of topics that have multiple viewpoints from which to argue (e.g., banning the sale of plastic straws and grocery bags or drilling for oil or minerals in the Arctic). The teacher probes with a few questions to get the pulse of how well the students understand the nature of the arguments presented.

The students are given an article to read that outlines some of the possible arguments, then they are permitted to choose a partner or triad with whom to work as they research their issue. They discuss the issues and jot down notes using the Cornell note-taking approach (Paulk, 2001) to identify the claims made in the article. Once they have finished the assignment, the students complete a short activity to think through how well they worked together (we call it the Goal 18 evaluation tool, and you can find it in Figure 5.13 on p. 100). Then they report what they found to the whole class. A rubric is given to the students that outlines the characteristics of effective arguments in writing and arguments that are suitable or may need improvement. The next day, students will use a graphic organizer to outline their arguments and begin writing. This lesson includes the tools, work products, and performances shown in Figure 2.3.

For discussion purposes, we use the term *tools* to refer to instruments that are intended to guide learning but are not the point of the learning; for example, the graphic organizer is not intended to be used as an end in and of itself; rather, it is used to help students organize their thinking. Work products are those artifacts that students create and that can be examined during production and at a later time. Performances are ephemeral and cannot be examined later. However,

Tools	Work products	Performances
		Responses to questions
		Discussion in pairs or triads
	Cornell notes	
		Goal 18
Rubric		
Graphic organizer		
	Written argument	

FIGURE 2.3. Artifacts, work products, and performances.

a teacher may choose to create anecdotal notes or an observation instrument that documents what information a performance might reveal.

We use the form in Appendix A, *Assessing the Assessments: Gathering Information and Evidence* (see pp. 167–169), to explore the assessment opportunities in the lesson. It's certainly possible to make an assessment by placing checkmarks in the matrix cells, which sometimes is enough, but a few keywords or notes can be helpful, too.

In the completed example in Figure 2.2, not all the cells in the matrix are checked upon because it is not necessary to use all the tools and activities in every lesson. As you can see, almost anything students do can produce assessment data even if that is not the primary purpose. For example, students may analyze an argument for the purpose of meeting the instructional objectives, but their analyses also provide information that the teacher can use to guide and adjust instruction.

Also note that each of the assessment sources in the matrix is coded to indicate whether it is primarily content (C), process (P), or product (Pr). Being precise by knowing what assessment information we are gathering can be helpful when it is time to act on the assessment information gathered.

INTERPRETING AND ANALYZING ASSESSMENT INFORMATION

Once evidence is gathered, we need to make sense of it. What do we have? What does it mean? Again, a chart may help us organize our thinking. Using the same example, the eighth-grade lesson on argumentation, we can parse the information and start planning our actions for adjusting instruction and providing feedback.

Before we jump in, we must first ask ourselves, how do we know students have learned? Put another way, how do we work with students to make learning visible? That age-old routine when Mom asks, "What did you learn in school today?" is instructive.

MOM: What did you learn in school today, Alex?

ALEX: Nothing. We read from some old book.

Sound familiar? Teaching students to make their learning visible (e.g., Fisher, Frey, & Hattie, 2016) flips that exchange on its head. What if Alex knew why he read that book? One "move" students might be taught to make is to be able to explain any learning task and how it fits into greater understanding.

Doug Fisher and Nancy Frey write about their journey to make literacy learning visible at an urban high school in Chapter 7 (see the box "Using Effect Sizes to Determine Impact and Adjust Learning Experiences" on pp. 138–140). For now, literacy consultant Angela Stockman (2015) suggests three moves that students should use to make their learning visible, and we have added our own to hers for a total of four:

1. Demonstrate or describe the purpose of any learning task and how it meets the standards and other measures of quality.
2. Explain and understand the process that resulted in their product.
3. Reflect before, during, and after learning.
4. Describe metacognitive moves (such as self-assessment or use of strategies).

If learning is made visible, then it is possible to better interpret and analyze assessment data. The form in Appendix B, *Assessing the Assessments: Interpreting and Analyzing Assessment Data* (see pp. 170–171), can be deployed in several ways. A teacher may use it to predict what information a planned assessment event provides or to assess the assessment events (yep, we assess our assessments to make sure they are of good quality). An observer might be invited to use the tool to help a teacher spot ways to improve classroom assessment, or students might use a modified version to reflect on what they learn, on how they learn, and on how they know they have learned. We give an example in Figure 2.4.

Another way to visualize the assessment and learning cycle is the feedback process cycle, which appears in Figure 2.5 (p. 29), and is produced by the Assessment Design Decisions project in Australia. You can read about the project's framework for assessment at *www.assessmentdecisions.org/framework*.

Assessment Checklist: Interpreting

Date: *February 6, 2020*

Teacher: *Mr. Yorick*

Class: *3rd period*

Observer: *n/a*

Subject: *English, 8th grade*

Standards: *CCSS.ELA-Literacy.W.7.1—Write arguments to support claims with clear reasons and relevant evidence.*

Student Learning Objective(s)	Type or Format of Assessment Source	Supporting Information
☐ Students will be able to identify and analyze the claims made in a written argument. ☑ Students will select and construct claims for an argument essay they will write.	☑ Questioning ☑ Discussion ☐ Quick assessment (e.g., exit slip) ☑ Written product ☑ Performance ☑ Observation ☑ Portfolio ☐ Other	☑ Rubric ☐ Checklist ☐ Scoring guide ☑ Models and exemplars ☑ Directions oral or written ☑ Other student materials (texts, computer, etc.) *Goal 18, Graphic organizer, Cornell notes, Model argument text*
Artifact or Performance represents ☐ Content ☑ Process ☑ Product	**Information obtained**	**Planned feedback**
Teacher effectively measures student learning in relation to learning objectives.	How do you know? *During questioning, students can deconstruct an argument from a text.* *Rubric is linked to key success indicators found in the standards and in model essays.*	**[To be explored in Chapter 4]**

(continued)

FIGURE 2.4. Completed example of Appendix B, Assessing the Assessments: *Interpreting and Analyzing Assessment Data.*

27

Student Learning Objective(s)	Type or Format of Assessment Source	Supporting Information
Teacher effectively measures student performance in relation to his/her performance at a prior time—Baseline assessment or data.	How do you know? *Students use work in their portfolio to estimate their progress toward increased writing proficiency.*	
Learning tasks and performances are appropriately complex relative to standards.	How do you know? *Students are able to explain the tasks relative to the learning objective and standards.* *Students can describe the purpose for each learning task.* *Students use the rubric and models to demonstrate their level of achievement.*	
Learning tasks provide appropriate challenge and guidance with visible progress indicators.	How do you know? *Graphic organizer, teacher observation of student work, and partner discussions offer progress indicators.* *Cornell notes offer the opportunity to make in-depth analysis of how well students are able to deconstruct an argument.*	

☐ Student ownership of learning evident.
  • Self-assessment
  • Peer assessment
	What evidence of ownership is available? *Students use the rubric to grade their own essays, identifying areas of strength and areas in need of improvement.*	

FIGURE 2.4. (*continued*)

Key considerations:
- How are multiple feedback opportunities achieved through the distribution and relationship of tasks across the unit/module/overall program?
- What types of feedback information will be provided and by whom?
- How will learner performance be used to influence the (re)design of later tasks?

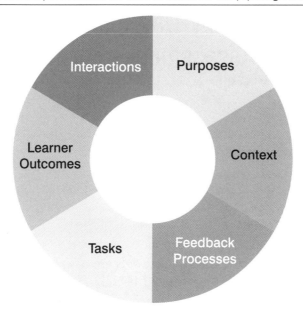

FIGURE 2.5. Feedback process cycle. Reprinted with permission from Assessment Design Decisions.

CHAPTER 3

Day-by-Day Teaching
with Assessment Information

Often, teachers see solid, time-tested ideas presented as something new. Maybe the package is new, the terms or buzzwords are new, or a policy highlights the (old) new idea. That's okay. Ideas should be subject to new scrutiny and novel ways to breathe new life where they had become stagnant or sometimes forgotten. "Understanding by design," "backward planning" (e.g., Wiggins & McTighe, 2005), "begin with the end in mind" (Covey, 1989), and "visible learning" (e.g., Fisher et al., 2016) all call attention to practices teachers have employed long before those terms were coined. New attention in the context of changing education environments is worthwhile, we think.

In an educational world filled with pacing guides and high-stakes exams for accountability, it can be a challenge to keep our focus as educators where it belongs: on student learning and engagement. Understanding by design, for example, reminds us that effective teaching means having a plan, designed with specific outcomes in mind, centered around how students learn and what their interests and needs are. Assessment literacy necessarily means knowing how to gather, use, and interpret assessment information as part of teaching and learning. Assessment, teaching, and learning are interwoven elements of the same story. Take one element out of the story, and the whole enterprise of education falls into a heap of pedagogical rubble.

Let's take a side trip for a moment and consider models. In education, we have models for many things, including lesson plans. In Figure 3.1, several lesson plan models are displayed side by side so that the elements can be compared.

While it is possible to take a lesson apart, the choice of what parts are most important is a decision made by the researcher or observer. For the most part, the elements are similar for all plans. For example, all of the plans have a provision for objectives, goals, and perhaps standards. Most have a provision for monitoring what

Hunter (1982): Mastery teaching	Cennamo, Ross, & Ertmer (2009): GAME Plan	Burke (2015)	National University (2010)	Serdyukov & Ryan (2008)
			• Description: name, supervisor, date, etc.	• Description
			• Introduction	
• Objectives	• Set goals	• Objectives	• Learner outcomes and objectives	• Goals and objectives
			• Preassessment activity	
			• Differentiation, adaptation, and accommodation	
		• Act I*	• Resources	• Materials and tools
• Anticipatory set • Input and modeling	• Take action	• Act II	• Teacher explicit instruction*	• Procedures introduction • New material presentation
• Checking for understanding and guided practice	• Monitor		• Guided or collaborative practice (provision for checking for understanding included)*	• Activities
• Independent practice		• Act III	• Independent practice*	
			• Closure	• Closure
	• Evaluate and extend	• Remember and reflect • Homework	• Reflective assessment	• Reflective assessment and clarification

FIGURE 3.1. Lesson plan format comparison chart. *Burke's (2015) model is based on the idea that a secondary class period of less than an hour should not be segmented into more than three parts or it will lose coherence.

students learn and how they are learning it. Often, an evaluation phase is included, though typically it is the last element in the deconstructed lesson.

CLASSROOM ASSESSMENTS

Classroom assessments tell the story of individual student progress. You, the teacher, will have the most control over decisions about assessing individual students. You can administer the assessments you select, or they can be used by students for self-assessment. As you consider different assessments, Ainsworth (2015, p. 30) suggests you follow this thinking process.

1. Know your purpose.
2. Determine the appropriate assessment that will accomplish your identified purpose.
3. Select or create a quality assessment.
4. Administer and score the assessment; analyze the assessment results.
5. Make an accurate inference.
6. Adjust instructional decisions in a timely manner.

The purposes are to measure the level of achievement on learning targets, either formatively or summatively. Teachers use classroom assessments to identify student strengths and weaknesses, to consider how well their instruction is being received, to monitor progress, to make adaptations to their lesson plans, and to give grades. Classroom assessments can also be used by students for self-assessment of their own learning progress and for setting goals.

Two decades ago, Black and Wiliam (1998) conducted a meta-analysis of studies on assessments and concluded that improving learning depends on five key factors:

1. The provision of effective feedback to students
2. The active involvement of students in their own learning
3. Adjusting teaching to take account of the results of assessments
4. A recognition of the profound influence assessment has on the motivation and self-esteem of students, both of which are crucial influences on learning
5. The need for students to be able to assess themselves and understand how to improve

We often think of classroom assessment in three ways: assessment *for* learning (formative), assessment *of* learning (summative), and assessment *as* learning (student self-assessment). As a classroom teacher, you'll want to include all three in your program.

Assessment *for* Learning: Formative Assessment

Assessment for learning involves teachers using assessment to inform their teaching, with the ultimate goal for both the teacher and the student of knowing what actions to take to keep the learning on track. Formative assessments are pragmatic; they are used to learn and adapt ongoing instruction. Formative assessment allows teachers to enter a dialogue with learners. This dialogue begins with the teacher. You are teaching a skill or concept, and you want to know if students are starting to grasp it. You are asking questions such as,

- "How well do students know this skill?"
- "Do I need to continue teaching this skill?"
- "Do I need to teach it a different way?"
- "Can I move on to the next skill?"

If the purpose of formative assessments is to inform teachers about the success of their instruction and to inform students about their learning progress, you need to consider several things as you develop them. First, you need to make sure your learning targets are clear, and you then need to have clear criteria for success. For example, let's say you were teaching students that stories have a beginning, middle, and end. Your learning target could be something like the following: Students will be able to identify the beginning, middle, and end of the story *The Paper Crane* (Bang, 1988) by drawing pictures of each of its components. Your criteria would be that students draw identifiable pictures of a very kind restaurant owner standing by his restaurant (beginning), a picture of a stranger with old clothes walking into the restaurant and giving the owner a paper crane (middle), and finally a picture of the paper crane coming to life (end). As you teach this skill, you might tell a familiar story, such as Little Red Riding Hood, and explain to students that the story has a beginning, middle, and end. You might then want to observe if students understood this concept through formative assessment by having them tell you or draw what they believe is the beginning of the story. As you walk around the room looking at students' drawings, you can get a sense of whether they understood your instruction or whether you need to provide them with a different example. This formative assessment is part of the instructional process before you determine whether students have begun to learn.

Assessment *of* Learning: Summative Assessments

After you have taught a skill or strategy, you will want to know whether students have actually learned it. This is assessment *of* learning, or summative assessments. Assessments themselves are not formative or summative; what matters is how they are used. Summative assessments inform you about the achievement status of the student, and they need to:

1. Mirror learning goals,
2. Measure knowledge, understandings, or skills,
3. Be aligned with cognitive level of learning goals, and
4. Have clear criteria.

Going back to our example from the previous section, you would be using a summative assessment when you read the book *The Paper Crane,* had students draw pictures, and graded the pictures students drew. After you were finished scoring the pictures, you then would interpret the data. As you can see, summative assessments don't need to be formal tests. They can be any kind of evaluation that measures students' learning at the end of a lesson or unit.

Assessment *as* Learning: Student Self-Assessment

We have used the metaphor of a story for the assessment process. As you think of formative and summative assessments, we'd like you to consider a third type of assessment, which is student self-assessment. In this type, students are given a voice in the assessment process. Giving students opportunities for self-assessment reminds Susan of Facebook alerts she occasionally gets: Jenna has added to her story. This is what we want students to do. As the teacher, you are tasked with the responsibility of directing your students' educational progress. You will be making many of the decisions and will be in charge of many of the activities. Ultimately, though, students need to take responsibility for their own learning, and you can help them by encouraging self-assessment.

Students can monitor their own learning through asking questions, reflecting, and goal setting. Even young children can ask questions, such as:

"Did I understand this?"
"What questions do I have to help me understand better?"
"What do I need to do to learn the next steps?"

In the example from the previous two sections using the learning target of understanding the beginning, middle, and end of stories, students can self-assess by comparing the pictures they drew to a model the teacher has provided. At that point, you could help students reflect on their learning by asking them to determine whether their pictures matched and whether they understood the concept.

Models are found in every discipline from education to science labs to archaeology, and each model is an attempt to recreate something far more complex. George

Box, a statistician, noted that "Essentially all models are wrong, but some are useful" (in Wasserstein, 2010). The lesson here is that any model of assessment, lesson design, or curriculum mapping is ultimately a deconstruction of what really occurs in classrooms. The extent to which each or any model represents what teachers instruct, what they plan, and what students learn is complex and should be considered for what it is and what its limitations are.

In their analysis of how models are useful (or not), Saltelli and Funtowicz (2014) suggest that rule one for the responsible use of models should be, "Use models to clarify, not to obscure" ("simpler models . . . , para. 1). Their second rule is equally valuable because it asks what assumptions support the foundations of the model. In the case of lesson plan models or templates, we teachers should understand that every model for a lesson highlights what the researcher was studying or what the template designer believed was important.

Spiro and colleagues (1996) suggested that cognitive flexibility theory is a useful framework for considering approaches to literacy instruction. Cognitive flexibility theory posits that ill-structured domains do not lend themselves well to reduction, to disaggregation, or to oversimplification. Writing, for example, may be better suited to what Spiro and colleagues call the expansive and flexible worldview that avoids prescriptive approaches or single representations of the product or process. Taken from this perspective, the most appropriate means of determining just how teachers interact with students, satisfy curricular requirements, and address the demands of academic writing is to observe students' writing in progress and then to use the written products as artifacts for discussion and analysis of the teaching processes that contributed to the students' interconnected understanding of writing in school.

 Trickster trap: Simplifying is not the same thing as making something simple. Students often respond to the complexity of a problem.

MODELS: THE DNA OF THE CLASSROOM

Models, whether they are representations of lesson plans, of theories of learning, or of objects from the physical world, can help us understand aspects of whatever the phenomenon happens to be. When I (Thomas) was much younger, I made real and imagined models of United States naval vessels, Air Force planes, historic tall ships, and space exploration vehicles. The starship *Enterprise* was displayed right next to the Apollo–Soyuz historic docking of spacecraft from two countries. Neither one of these model spacecraft would ever be propelled into orbit around Earth or any other planet, but the models were useful to me. From them, I gained an understanding of the art of science fiction and the science involved in melding technologies that were not completely compatible.

Throughout this book, we make the case that assessment and instruction are integrally connected and that a model can help us visualize this connection. A quick review of classroom assessments can help inform our understanding of the model, though.

My model of an F-16 aircraft built of plastic could never fly, but building it did help me understand the principles of aerodynamics and imagine a world where I might be a pilot someday. The engines would never produce the thrust necessary to overcome gravity, but they could help me visualize the role of the real thing in doing so. What we educators need is a model that does not separate assessment from teaching and learning. Assessment that tells a story has to be integral to the act of teaching and learning to be useful.

Fortunately, such a model is literally found in our DNA. DNA (deoxyribonucleic acid), as described by James Watson and Francis Crick (1953), is a double helix constructed of sugar-phosphate backbones joined together by hydrogen bonds and pairs of nitrogenous bases.[1] We borrowed the double-helix model to show the relationship between instruction and assessment, particularly formative assessments—the DNA of the classroom (see Figure 3.2). In our representation, assessment information is gathered simultaneously, or nearly so, while teaching proceeds. Teachers check for understanding and use that information to provide useful feedback to students about their performance.

TEACHING AND LEARNING

How information and learning activities are organized (Hunter, 1982) is vitally important, so our lesson plans should reflect care and attention. Students may struggle to transfer knowledge from one domain to another, but a well-designed lesson can help them do so.

Gick and Holyoak (1983) found that even graduate students struggle to apply strategic knowledge that is familiar to them in an unfamiliar new domain. Participants in their experiments were presented with a scenario and a solution in one domain (the military), but they did not easily transfer the attributes of the first scenario and solution to a new domain (medicine), even though the strategy was the same for both problems.

Teachers encounter this phenomenon regularly. Students who seem to master a concept on Monday struggle with the same skill or concept under somewhat different conditions on Wednesday. Better organization of the learning activities is part of the solution. Difficult concepts, according to CAST (2011), should be presented in multiple ways and through many encounters. If we teach in this way, students

---

[1] Learn more about the discovery of the double helix at *https://profiles.nlm.nih.gov/SC/Views/Exhibit/narrative/doublehelix.html*.

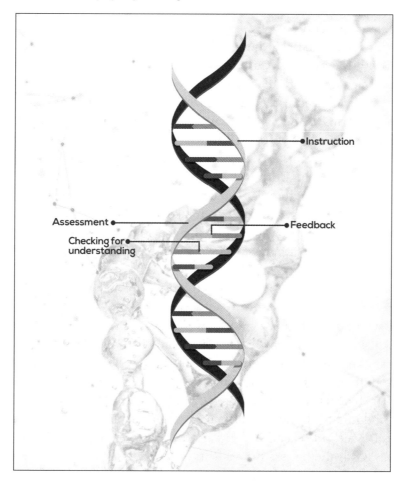

FIGURE 3.2. Instruction and assessment: the DNA of the classroom.

are more likely to have learned deeply and are able to transfer knowledge. Any discussion of assessment, according to our DNA of learning model, must include examination of the instructional processes and the learning that is to be assessed.

INSTRUCTION

So, what is instruction? Durkin (1990) thought of instruction as "what someone or something does or says that has the potential to teach one or more individuals what they do not know, do not understand, or cannot do" (p. 472). She explains that direct instruction can be planned or unplanned; it can be part of a small-group instructional plan or a lesson for the whole class (Durkin, 1981). When an unanticipated learning situation arises, direct instruction may also be something the teacher does in that moment.

Typically, instruction involves providing some type of input with which students will interact. Often, that instruction includes directions about what students should do with the material. Care must be taken that students understand what they are expected to do with the input. The use of models is one way to accomplish the clarity students need if they are to achieve the learning target. Models take many different forms. Let's look at some examples.

Ms. Hicken (a pseudonym, like the other teacher names in this chapter) teaches fourth grade, and she wants her students to work in groups. Since her classroom is equipped with individual desks arranged in rows, students must move their desks into a different formation in order to work with their team. This can end up being noisy and time-consuming, so Ms. Hicken takes the time to model exactly how to pick up a desk, to turn it toward the group, and to sit back down. She physically picks up the desk, turns it, and sits down again, so students can see how quickly and relatively quietly the task can be accomplished. Now, she and her students can spend more time actually learning in groups, instead of making the transition from rows to groupwork.

Mr. Bennett teaches eighth grade. His students are working on an analysis of a novel they have just read. Mr. Bennett distributes to the students copies of a well-written essay analyzing a different novel. Fortunately, he saved some examples of student work from earlier years; his students seem to relate to essays that are written by other students more than those written by professionals. The students read the essay and find the features that make it exemplary. In fact, Mr. Bennett calls this type of model an "exemplar." He also distributes some other essays that are not quite as good, and he asks his students to examine them and decide how these essays might be improved. He calls these models "anchors" because they also are examples that are linked to the rubric the students use as they write. We explore rubrics in more detail in another chapter.

Mrs. Bradley has noticed that her third graders continuously misspell the word *cemetery* as "cemetary" during their Halloween story writing activity. She knows that if she tells them not to make that mistake, a few will correct their misspellings, but most will forget in the moment they need it because they are more involved in writing the story. Her solution is easy and involves a model. She writes "cemetary" on the board and draws a big red X over it. Then she writes *cemetery* in large letters, and she leaves the word there while students are writing. Mrs. Bradley tells her students that they may not misspell the word *cemetery* any longer because it is right in front of them on the board in large letters. As she monitors her students' work, Mrs. Bradley notices that Ahmed has forgotten how to spell the word, so she puts her finger on the mistake on Ahmed's paper and points to the board. Ahmed knows what that means: it's time to fix the error.

Mr. Davies teaches a terrific group of high school juniors in his science class, and they are reading an article from a science journal before proceeding to the lab area to conduct an experiment. He knows that the students will complete the reading at different paces, so he writes a set of instructions on the board (sometimes he projects these on a PowerPoint slide), so students have a reference for what they should do and in what order. The written instructions are a type of model that keeps the class moving along smoothly.

1. "When you finish reading the article, write one paragraph applying the concept from that article to the experiment you are about to conduct."
2. "Ask Mr. Davies or the lab assistant to approve your paragraph."
3. "Proceed quietly to the lab area and set up the equipment needed for the experiment."
4. "Begin the experiment when all of your team members arrive at the lab station."

In each of these teaching examples, a model helps students understand what they are to do and how they are to interact with the information or input provided. Ms. Hicken uses a model to help her students with a routine that will make their use of class time more efficient. Mr. Bennett uses exemplars and anchors to provide students models of a complex writing task, and he helps them identify the key features of those models, so students can use them to inform their own writing.

Mrs. Bradley uses a simple model to help students learn to attend to the spelling of challenging words and reminds them that since the word is right in front of them, they need only look up and check their spelling against hers. Mr. Davies facilitates the reading and lab assignments by providing written directions. If a student forgets what to do and goes off task, all Mr. Davies has to do is get the students' attention and point to the board where the directions are written.

Effective models play an important part in assessment, as we soon see. They provide a point of reference, so students know what high-quality work looks like. However, models do come with some traps teachers can avoid as well.

Trickster trap 1: A model that is precisely like the intended outcome may encourage students to perfunctorily mimic the model. In Mr. Bennett's class, his students use models of essays for a different novel than the book they are reading. In so doing, they attend to the features of the analysis, rather than mimicking the language and style of the original models.

Trickster trap 2: Models that are representative of complex processes or products can be confusing to students if they don't know what aspects of the model are important. Stephen Covey (1989), in his famous book *The Seven Habits of Highly Effective People,* recounts the story of his son who was learning to take care of the yard. His son agreed to take on the job of keeping the yard at their house green and clean. Using a neighbor's green and clean yard as a model, Stephen and his son started working together on the yard. But day after day, the family's yard became less green and less clean. When Stephen asked his son why the task was not done, he responded that it was just too hard. What Stephen realized was that the job was actually overwhelming, and he still needed to help his son until he could see that the yard was becoming green and clean under his stewardship. Just because there is a model does not mean students will not need additional support.

 Trickster trap 3: A single model may induce students to copy its features exactly without understanding how or why the model is effective. Instead, provide several models that show how the concept or skill is used in different contexts.

TEACHER PRESENTATIONS AND LECTURE

Teacher presentations and lecture can be an important part of learning, even though lecture has gotten a bad rap sometimes (e.g. Bransford, Brown, & Cocking, 2000). At the same time, Freire (1970/1993) reminds us that a banking approach to education is problematic. In the banking approach, the teacher has all the knowledge, and her job is to fill the students' heads with what she knows. Banking knowledge makes the teacher the actor (the person who engages in action) and the students the passive recipients. The students are not in control of their own learning. Lecture has a place in learning, but we also think that banking knowledge can become a default teaching method that excludes what students can do to promote their own learning.

MODELS AND TEACHERS: A TEACHER LEADER PRO TIP

Recently, a teacher in Guatemala—we will call him Juan—was working diligently to use *constructivist*, student-centered approaches to his teaching. His successes led other teachers to emulate what he was doing. However, Juan was stymied when it came to teaching students to use punctuation. He followed traditional approaches that emphasized rules, and they just weren't working. What Juan needed was a model of how to teach punctuation as a constructivist. If you are wondering how this model worked, we can explain. Juan and I (Thomas) discussed how it was done—in Spanish, of course.

We can use a workshop approach to learning how to use commas and other punctuation. Sometimes learning needs to be shaped specifically, and it can be done through a constructivist approach, in the case of using commas, just as other learning can. Let us say that we want to teach students to use commas in a series. We could (we *shouldn't,* but we could) just teach the rule: Use commas to separate words and word groups in a simple series of three or more items. However, students might say that they understand the rule, but that they usually can't apply it when they write. Thus, we have a problem. The teacher can say, "I TOLD you that commas are placed after items in a series, so why didn't you do that here?" (Frustration on everyone's part.)

Given that our research on the "interwebs" indicates that commas in English and Spanish are used in roughly analogous ways, here is how we would proceed. Consider these three arbitrary whole sentences (emphasis on *whole*):

The red fox jumped over the fence.
The brown bear jumped over the fence.
The tan deer jumped over the fence.

Students will now say, "Boring." And they will be right, so we say, "Well, what can we do about this?" Students, smart pupils that they are, notice that the red fox, brown bear, and tan deer are all in the adjective–noun form and everything else is identical. Now, and this is important, the students might not be able to say that red, brown, and tan are colors used as adjectives, and they might not be able to tell me that the fox, bear, and deer are nouns. But their smart, language-learning brains know this, even if they can't tell me how the words are classified by grammarians, by English-Spanish teachers, and by that persistent nun with a ruler ready to pounce on anyone who is not familiar with the concept of the present participle.

Our creative students (that's *all* of them) immediately recognize the pattern even if they don't know the rule. They *combine* the sentences because sentences are all about ideas and humans are very good at shaping ideas. This is where the fun and learning begin because we are not talking about comma splices and run-on sentences here (you know, rules). We are going to avoid these rules through this approach. Rather, the students are going to draw on the ideas that serve as a kind of foundation for language. By the way, this whole approach is based on the theories of Noam Chomsky (when he was more interested in linguistics than the language of politics) known as transformational-generative grammar. It was refined by William Strong into the approach known as sentence combining. Anyway, back to our students.

The students realized that the three sentences can be combined into something more elegant, and they produce this sentence:

The red fox, the brown bear, and the tan deer jumped over the fence.

Voila. They successfully manipulated the ideas into a sentence that in most cases is far better than the original three. Here we find our key: Spoken aloud, the new sentence is automatically punctuated through inflection. When written down, we have to separate the noun phrases with a comma. Simple as that, the students have learned how to punctuate nouns in a sentence. No boring rules, no teacher-led lectures, and no worksheets that would put a sloth to sleep. After a bit of practice in the same vein, they will be able to separate verb phrases, adjectives, clauses, and more. The more of this they do, the better they will understand the concept: Commas separate various elements of some types of sentences. Of course, there is more fun when they learn that commas can also enclose or contain elements of sentences, too.

This approach can be demonstrated to any group of students you choose. It's effective, it's kind of fun, and it's what a constructivist would do. (See what we did there?)

PRACTICE

Teaching that guides students to engage in learning requires lots of practice: guided practice, independent practice, group or team practice, rehearsals, repetitions, and trial runs. Practice is where formative assessment can make a substantial impact on the learner; that is, it can make a substantial impact if the teacher structures practice correctly. In our work with teachers and teachers to be, we have seen some amazing teaching. We can't really discuss classroom assessment unless we consider the activities that lead to learning in the first place.

One teacher we observed, Mr. Pascual, understood exactly what practice is intended to do—improve performance. Mr. Pascual asked his fifth-grade students to practice all kinds of things, and often. Writing? Yep, lots of it. Reading skills? You bet. When students were practicing, Mr. Pascual spent his time interacting with them in small groups and as individuals. (We get to this kind of teacher–student interaction in the next chapter.) What Mr. Pascual did was—gasp!—post the answers to whatever the students were practicing.

You might think that the students would go to the answers straightaway and just copy them, but that is not what happened. The fifth graders practiced and then looked at the answers to see how they did. When they found they had made mistakes, they went back to their desks to figure out why or where the errors had occurred. Think about that for a while: Why would students do that? The answer is simple. Mr. Pascual had normalized error. It's okay to make a mistake, and when you do, to go figure out why. Mr. Pascual had also conveyed that there was no penalty for making a mistake. Practice was intended as practice, not as a way to record grades that separate students into categories. You know which ones, A, B–, C, D+, and so on. We find that teachers who are at the top of their game make use of three tips, and they avoid two practice traps. Let's look at each of them.

Wise teacher tip: *Practice the right skills.* Even experts need practice, and they choose their practice carefully. A skilled teacher of reading still stops and reflects to refine her approach. She may find that some students need more practice with letter–sound correspondence even though she has already taught it. Perhaps she notices that her lessons are a little dated and in need of upgrading and revision. In the first case, the teacher would identify what activities would help the students succeed with this early reading skill, then she would practice the activity with another teacher, her young son, or her spouse.

A key tip for designing practice is knowing what exactly needs to be practiced. Some activities are practiced by the whole class, others in small groups, and others on an individual basis. Lemov, Woolway, and Yezzi (2012) use sports to distinguish between practice through drills and practice through scrimmage. Teachers sometimes shy away from "drill," and we have likely all used the phrase *drill and kill* from time to time. Drill that is pointless or just make-work deserves to be avoided, but drills that help students refine their skills and their understanding can be beneficial. Whereas scrimmage replicates an activity for practice, drill distorts it so that the facets of the skill are visible.

This distinction is useful in the classroom. Mrs. Webb teaches first grade. Her students need practice using morphemes to improve their comprehension during reading. Using words students know (e.g., telephone, microscope), she isolates the morpheme that builds to words students may not know. That's drill. Scrimmage involves having students read a text containing challenging words that require them to identify the morphemes to make sense of the passage. The challenge is determining exactly which skills students need, and that's where assessment comes into play. We return to this idea in the next chapter.

Wise teacher tip: *Practice can be fun.* A little competition can go a long way, as long as students stay focused on the skill or learning at hand. For example, competitive reading activities, such as "popcorn" reading (Wolsey, Lapp, & Dow, 2010), are popular all around the world. It is a practice activity that can be enjoyable and that looks like reading, but it is not. For those who may not know, popcorn reading and other competitive reading strategies involve variations of a student reading aloud, then suddenly calling the name of another student to read. The second student must pick up reading on the exact word where the previous student left off. We believe that this practice is actually a poor one because popcorn reading includes a stimulus–response error. Here is how that plays out. The teacher's goal for students is to read and follow along, but the students misunderstand the goal and believe their job is to avoid being caught on the wrong word. By misunderstanding the goal, students read word by word, defeating any efforts to read with more fluency.

On the other hand, practice that keeps the focus on the actual task can be very useful. Many teachers use Popsicle sticks, tongue depressors, or index cards with the students' names on them. These chits are used to ask students questions without relying on the students who have their hands up. Ask a question, pull a card or stick, and ask the student whose name appears to respond to the question. If everyone knows the information, then it is more than fair to call on any of the students.

One teacher used the cards for review by following the format of the game show "Who Wants to Be a Millionaire?" On asking a question, he then drew a card and asked the person whose name was on it to respond. Notice that the question is asked before the student's name is called. Students could use a lifeline, as in the game show, if they struggle with the answer. However, instead of phoning a friend, they were permitted to ask any other student in class for help before providing the answer. In all cases, the student who was called upon had to provide the answer, though, and verify that they agreed or not with the friend they "phoned." Students were also permitted to poll the audience by asking the rest of the class for a show of hands or to ask an expert (which meant they could look through their notes or textbooks).

 Wise teacher tip: *Make time to practice.* With all that teachers must do these days, it can be easy to cover material without providing the practice students need to really learn well. We have found that teachers who achieve good results are those who know how to design practice and make sure that there is time for it.

 Sage leader tip: Teacher leaders (principals, instructional coaches, or mentors) can help teachers normalize practice by providing time for teachers to practice their craft as well. If practice helps students achieve, it can also help teachers achieve—if time and opportunity make it possible. When Mrs. Everest's fifth-grade student still struggles to comprehend what he reads, she may schedule a parent conference, one that is sure to be uncomfortable for everyone. Her principal, Mr. Lamb, can help by inviting her to his office to practice what needs to be said and how the conference might unfold. When practice is expected of everyone at school, everyone, whatever their role, achieves more effectively.

 Trickster trap: *Practice makes perfect.* Most of us have heard this aphorism before, and maybe the response to it: Practice makes permanent. Imperfect practice leads to persistent errors that are very difficult to correct. This is one reason why thoughtfully designed learning objectives are imperative. Reading, for example, is often sidetracked when students internalize a common prompt: If you don't know a word, just skip it. If students learn to skip the word, but not figure it out or to return to it and figure it out, their reading problems will multiply as they move from grade to grade and into adult life. Perfectly designed practice makes perfect.

Trickster trap: *Practice is not a punishment.* In the second wise teacher tip, we suggested that practice can be fun. The opposite is also true: If students come to abhor practice, they will not do it very well. Some of our readers will recall being asked to copy long lists of vocabulary words and their definitions from the dictionary. Sheer drudgery, and ineffective to boot. Practice that is focused and has a clear purpose is much more likely to result in engaged students.

STORIES FROM THE CLASSROOM

Coaches and students in physical education courses use complex vocabulary and communication all the time. Bryan Fisher teaches Physical Education at Pinole Middle School in the West Contra Costa Unified School District in California. He shares strategies for assessing vocabulary and critical thinking skills.

Assessment of Academic Vocabulary and Understanding in Secondary Physical Education

Bryan Fisher

Checking for understanding is a universal necessity in every discipline of education. Contrary to popular belief, the discipline of physical education is no different, however unique it may be. As a physical educator over the past 4 years, I have accumulated a wealth of experience in what it means to assess students in my class fairly, reasonably, and without taking away their actual need for a break from the classroom setting when they come to my course. In this writing, I share what I have found to be the most effective assessments of students' knowledge, as they pertain to academic vocabulary in physical education.

Direct Observation of Physical Response to Auditory Cues

The most common technique used in my class is direct observation. Since our class is usually outdoors, and I have to physically carry any materials on my person, I have learned to rely on this approach. You may wish to use a written checklist; however, if the checklist is short you can simply hold the information in your memory while observing student performance.

The first example of physical response can be in the form of having students orally recite the biomechanical terms or cues for completing various tasks while performing the corresponding physical action. Students must know each cue, in the proper order, and demonstrate each one correctly. For example, if we begin with the jump shot, the cues would be something like: "shoulder width" (base), "45 degree" (knees), "aim and fire" (elbow), "follow through." This assessment is preceded by a lecture in which students are asked to perform and recite the cues as a class and with the teacher. The assessment can be performed individually, but I highly recommend assessing in small groups because of class size and limited time. This is a play-off of a strategy called total physical response (TPR).

WRITTEN RESPONSE TO IMAGES

Visual aids have been shown to have a positive impact on student learning. Some students are auditory learners, some are kinesthetic learners, yet others are visual/observational learners. Figure 3.3 shows several images of a cartoon referee performing various hand signals for common basketball violations. This assessment is preceded by an introduction to rule-violation signals, in which the teacher performs signals and students mimic and verbally recite the name of the violation.

CRITICAL THINKING IN PHYSICAL EDUCATION

One of the more difficult concepts to incorporate was the aspect of critical thinking in physical education and how to assess it. I found that the most effective way to assess student critical thinking skills was to introduce the strategy to students by asking them to recognize when to utilize a certain technique, depending on what scenario is presented during a game. For example, in basketball students can be taught multiple types of defense, as well as what type of offensive play or move strategically provides an advantage. The most effective way that I have found to assess student critical thinking skills is to distribute blank index cards that have a multiple-part question that allows students to display their logic and reasoning. For example, I may conduct a two-on-two modified drill midway through a 3-week unit. During the reflection period toward the end of the class, I may ask students to describe a pass (bounce pass, chest pass, lob pass, etc.) that they made during the modified drill, why they chose that pass, and the conditions that made them decide on that pass. This drill can be done verbally, but I prefer asking for written responses to allow adequate time for the students to think about their responses.

Physical Education: Mr. Fisher

Rules and violation signals

1. If a player moves while in possession of the ball without dribbling, it is called
   _____.

2. If a player takes too long to inbound the ball, it is called a
   _____.

3. If an offensive player dribbles with both hands at the same time, he has
   committed a _____ violation.

4. If a player who possesses the ball goes from across the half court line then
   back again, it is called a _____ violation.

5. If an offensive player runs into a deffender with an established position, it is a
   _____ violation.

6. When a defender stands in the key for too long, it is called a
   _____ violation.

FIGURE 3.3. Sample assessment using written responses to images. Reprinted with permission from Bryan Fisher.

CHAPTER 4

The Bond between Instruction and Assessment
The DNA of the Classroom

In our model based on the double helix (see Figure 3.2 on p. 37), we postulate that assessment and instruction are integral and parallel processes. What binds one strand to the other in the classroom? Checking for understanding and feedback. Let's examine each of these ideas.

CHECKING FOR UNDERSTANDING

Does everyone understand? Are there any questions? Teachers know instinctively that it is a good idea to make sure everyone understands the directions, the skills, and the concepts. The real challenge is knowing how to check for understanding. As we saw in Bryan Fisher's story at the end of Chapter 3, it's an art that effective teachers use. It's also a classroom assessment practice.

One of the easiest tools in the checking for understanding arsenal is walking around. Yes, that's right, walking around. Good managers do it, effective school principals do it, and teachers do it as well (Peters & Waterman, 2004). The best time to identify a mistake or a learning opportunity is while the students are working on whatever the product or process is. We avoid the terms *walking and stalking* and *monitoring* because these terms suggest distrust in our students. Stalking suggests that if we don't sneak up, the students will see us coming and modify their behavior, while monitoring seems to be what is needed to ensure compliance, not learning.

Checking for understanding, on the other hand, implies just what it states. By walking around, teachers can spot what students do or do not understand or comprehend. There is a challenge with checking for understanding by walking around, though. Consider the following scenario.

Praise, Prompt, and Leave

Ms. Carter (we're using pseudonyms again) has just released her students to begin working on an opinion essay after presenting the task and providing instruction via models of good opinion writing and analysis in small groups. She asks "Are there any questions?" and there are not, other than "How long does this have to be?" However, as soon as the students start to work, five hands go up, and Ms. Carter moves from one to the next. While the other four students' hands are in the air waiting for Ms. Carter to come to their rescue, they are also not writing. In fact, the hand with the pen is usually the one that is in the air. It's a dodge, an artful one, on the part of the students. It looks like interest in the task, but it is also means they do not need to work as long as their hand is up. Yikes. Something has to be done, and her principal, Mrs. Demostrar, shows her a technique that works like a charm. It is called "praise, prompt, and leave" (Jones, 2007).

With the instructional objective in mind and the success criteria for the task on a rubric, Ms. Carter moves from student to student, or group to group, offering a word of specific praise linked to that objective. She avoids generic praise (good job!) that offers no useful feedback. Next, she prompts the student to correct errors and suggests an alternate method or another way to move forward on this task or on a future activity.

Mrs. Demostrar is no ordinary principal, and she goes beyond just telling Ms. Carter about the strategy (remember the pro tip for teacher leaders in the last chapter?). In her office, after school, Mrs. Demostrar and Ms. Carter role-play how praise, prompt, and leave works. She offers to demonstrate the technique in class the next day. When she arrives, Ms. Carter welcomes the principal to the classroom. She explains that she is trying a new technique that the principal will demonstrate, and she needs her students' help.

Mrs. Demostrar digs right in. She tells the students that today, except in an emergency, they are not to raise their hands as they work on the opinion essay. Instead, she and Ms. Carter will stop by each of their desks and chat about their work. Each interaction is short, and Mrs. Demostrar and Ms. Carter give one specific positive comment about each student's work. They also point out one possible next step (the prompt), and then they move on. In time, Ms. Carter realizes she can interact with each student easily if she keeps her comments short and specific. Here is what the technique looks like.

> MRS. DEMOSTRAR: Manuel, I noticed your lead-in, your introduction, to this opinion piece is creative, using an anecdote from your own life. [Praise]
>
> MANUEL: Cool, thanks, Mrs. Demostrar. I wondered if this story would catch your eye.

MRS. DEMOSTRAR: One thing you can consider, moving forward, is to build on that story at this point in the essay. See? (*Puts her finger on the page to show where.*) [Prompt]

MANUEL: I like that idea!

MRS. DEMOSTRAR: (*Leaves and moves on to the next student.*)

[Meanwhile, Mary puts her hand up. Ms. Carter reminds her that she or Mrs. Demostrar will be around soon.]

MS. CARTER: Mary, please put your hand down and keep working on the parts you understand. Mrs. Demostrar or I will be there soon.

Like the index cards (or Popsicle sticks) with students' names on them, praise, prompt, and leave puts the responsibility for learning on the student. It is not possible to opt out by putting your hand up or muttering, "I don't know." The teacher is now free to check all students' understanding, and all of the students benefit from interaction with the teacher. Morale and trust are built at the same time. Now that's a win–win scenario.

More Ways to Check

Red Cup, Green Cup

When one of us (Thomas) was a newly minted teacher, he was assigned to work with English language learners in an urban middle school (it was known as an intermediate school in those days). The students were all over the place in terms of their language proficiency, and even with a paraeducator to help, the assignment was a tough one for a brand-new teacher. Working with Mrs. Matthews, a mentor teacher, we devised a system of checking that addressed the fact that students were at many different levels of proficiency in the curriculum. Students were given plastic cups, the kind used at picnics, in red and green. Students who displayed the green cup were working and needed no help. Students who placed the red cup over the green one were ready for the teacher or the paraeducator to check their work. The system worked beautifully because the students were responsible for doing their best, freeing the teacher to work with small groups and the paraeducator to check students' understanding of their work.

Thumbs Up!

Most teachers have used this method or a variation of it from time to time. "Ready to work? Thumbs up. Need more assistance? Thumbs sideways. Totally lost? Thumbs down." Or this variation: "How many *r* sounds do you hear when I pronounce the word *library*? Hold up one finger if you hear one, two if you hear two, three if you hear three, and so on."

Exit Ticket

A popular strategy that works when it is structured well is the exit ticket. A well-designed exit ticket offers teachers the opportunity to learn what their students know, how they know it, and when it's time to teach the concepts again. We show an example of an exit ticket in Figure 4.1.

When a student completes an exit slip or ticket, she is reconfirming her understanding by reflecting what she learned in class and where she might still be confused. However, the teacher also has a window into what students grasp and what may warrant further instruction. Exit tickets are typically completed in just a few minutes and handed to the teacher as the students leave the classroom. Teachers can then review the students' responses and adjust instruction or correct misconceptions the next day, as well as build on students' insights. Teachers may also differentiate instruction based on the responses the students provide. By the way, in some cases it may be possible to use "entrance" tickets. What do you think the possibilities might be? We have compiled several (but by no means all) types of exit tickets in Figure 4.2.

 Magician tip 1: You may have seen Sean Bean in *The Fellowship of the Ring* in memes of all kinds with pithy sayings. "One does not simply . . .

> . . . eat one potato chip
> . . . ignore my text message
> . . . resist bacon
> . . . get an 'A' in my class"

We would love to show you one of these memes but, you know, copyright issues are involved. Still you likely know what we mean. If not, just Google "One does not simply . . ." and you will get it. The point is that exit slips (or *"Do it now"* at the beginning of class) are a good way to help students synthesize what they have learned and provide assessment information to the teacher. Many tools available online make creating memes easy. Introduce your students to Canva or Adobe Spark, and challenge them to find an image and create a meme representing the

Name:	Date:
The big idea today is . . .	
But I still wonder why . . .	

FIGURE 4.1. Example of an exit ticket.

The list	3 things I learned: 2 things I wonder about: 1 question I still have:
The imaginary friend	Your best friend was absent from class yesterday. What does she need to know to catch up?
Thinking about thinking (metacognition)	How do you think you did on the examination today? Why do you think so?
Cognitive strategies focus	In what ways were you able to use [name a cognitive strategy, e.g., summarization] to better understand the short story we read today?
The teacher tool	One thing Dr. Wolsey does that helps me learn is: And one thing he could do to help me learn more effectively is:
The survey	Please rank the following skills in order from the one you most need to work on to the area of least need: ____ Brainstorming ideas for writing ____ Writing the first draft ____ Revising what I wrote (I love my words!) ____ Editing for spelling, punctuation, and so on ____ Completing my final writing and submitting it

FIGURE 4.2. Types of exit tickets.

day's lesson. They may send the meme to you in a learning management system (e.g., Blackboard, Cornerstone, Google Classroom), Tweet it, or even email it to you. Try it—you will be amazed at what your students create.

 Magician tip 2: Smartphones are often put to good use in tech-savvy classrooms. Kahoot!, Socrative, and Nearpod allow students to submit responses to the teacher, who compiles them for display on the screen or interactive smart board. Students can use the results to guide discussion and correct misunderstandings (e.g., Burns, 2017).

Oops!: Responding to Student Errors

Our colleagues Doug Fisher and Nancy Frey (2014) (you will meet them again later in this book) suggest that an error is different from a mistake. Mistakes occur due to a lack of attention where it needs to be. For example, a teacher might forget to upload an article that she has asked students to read. The mistake is easily correctable once the students point it out! An error, on the other hand, occurs when a learner does not know, or is not sure about, what to do. Knowing what the underlying cause of the error is can help a teacher address the problem with precision.

Figure 4.3 lists common types of student errors and models some teacher responses for each type. First there are *factual errors*. Many students (and adults) hold the mistaken belief that the moon only comes out at night. That's a factual error that can confuse students when they are reading books on astronomy topics or reading fiction in which the moon is visible during the day.

Procedural errors occur when students mix up or omit steps in a process. In writing, students often confuse writing processes such as editing and revising. Each has specific purposes, and sometimes they overlap, but when editing is confused with revising, only a superficial examination of the structure of the essay with a few spelling errors or punctuation mistakes are corrected. By the way, did you see what we did there?

Transformational errors happen when students generalize a rule from one context or situation to another. One of the problems we see with formulaic writing (the five-paragraph essay and similar structures) is that students come to understand that these writing formats are used pretty much everywhere, even when different contexts suggest otherwise.

Students reading about Native Americans in the Southwest may be confused by their perception that all Native Americans lived in teepees. Errors of this type are *misconceptions*.

Transcription errors occur when students copy down information inaccurately. A student may say, "It's right here in my notes; you wanted us to write a 51-page essay," when the teacher actually suggested that about five pages should be sufficient.

Type	Student error	Possible teacher response
Factual errors	In a rough draft: "Thomas Jefferson authorized the transcontinental railroad in 1855."	"Farida, I'm glad you noticed how important the transcontinental railroad was. For just a moment, flip to this chart showing when President Jefferson was in office. What do you think?"
Procedural errors	English language learner: "I sitted down and started to work."	"Karim, you have a good grasp of the past tense. There are some exceptions to the use of -ed, though. What do you notice on this chart of irregular verbs about sitting?"
Transformational errors	"Ms. Hicken told us to skip words we don't know when we read out loud."	"Right, Shellie. Sometimes teachers ask students to skip words when they are reading aloud for others. But when you are reading aloud for yourself, it is a good idea to look back at the word and try to figure it out. What does the root phon mean as in this example: xylophone?"
Misconceptions	In a speech for a debate class: "Some vaccines have been shown to cause autism."	"There are some people who believe that vaccinations cause autism, Jayden. Remember our discussion about finding counterarguments? What were you able to locate?"
Transcription errors	On a student's lecture notes: "Stephen Douglas was an outspoken reformer and abolitionist."	"Andrew, there may have been more than one person with the name Douglas at the time, perhaps with different spellings. Let's take a look at the index to this book to learn if there are any mistakes here."

FIGURE 4.3. Responding to error types.

When teachers check for understanding, they increase the chances that students are able to correct the problem in the moment or as close to it as possible. You may remember having a paper handed back to you in high school or college, and you flipped right to the end to see what the final grade assigned was. Our students do this, too. The best time to make course corrections, address errors, and catch mistakes is while the process is under way or the product is still being created.

The principle of checking for understanding is that it has to occur as close as possible to the practice activity. Checking for understanding on the unit exam or final portfolio is too late. By that time, students do not have the opportunity to make any corrections or adjustments, and they have no incentive to do so.

An inability to do timely checking, too, is one of the many problems with most types of homework. Tasks completed at home are often scrutinized by the teacher much too late to obtain any meaningful check for understanding. There is little students could do with any feedback provided, and any information about errors or mistakes they made is too little, too late.

Read Up, Ask Around, Double-Check

One key to success when checking for understanding is having a framework that students can use to guide their own learning. In this way, students learn to rely on themselves, but know that they can check with others when the need arises. Promoting ownership means also knowing when and whom to ask for help. We use *read up, ask around, double-check* (Wolsey, 2014) as a way to provide students a framework for thinking about citing sources and being accurate in their writing, speaking, and multimedia projects.

Read up, ask around, double-check offers students a simple way to remember what they need to do to make their writing and other public work (such as a Google Slides show) accurate and noteworthy. Students can be experts if they know what expertise looks like. These include the skills of knowing through reading, asking for more information, and then checking twice for accuracy. Here is how it works.

Experts read lots of materials in their own fields and about other interests as well. In other words, they read widely but also for specific purposes. For example, while writing this book, we read or reread to make sure our information was accurate. In creating Figure 4.3, for example, we reread Fisher and Frey (2014) and compared the types of errors the authors noted with other sources. That is how we found a fifth error type, transcription errors.

We like to think that experts have all the answers, but real experts know the limits of their knowledge. When they need to make a connection to their own work or to learn something new, they do not hesitate to reach out to another person to ask. Teaching students to ask their peers who have particular skills or knowledge is a good start. In language arts, students can ask a peer nearby, "Do you think I need a comma here?" Or, "I know you water-ski on the weekends. Please tell me if you think my description of this competition sounds realistic."

It has never been easier to find an expert than it is now. An email or discussion forum allows anyone with an Internet connection to find virtually anyone else with a connection and ask a question. Pavan, a teaching colleague in New Jersey, connects her classroom of fifth graders to authors of their favorite books and to other classes across the continent to work together on science projects via Skype.

Finally, when a young author finishes a draft, teachers can help them by encouraging them to put the draft away until the next day. In a day or so, students can then be asked to reread their work to look for factual errors, punctuation mistakes, and so on. Slow writing means taking whatever time is necessary and creating a culture where time is on the author's side to check the details. Giving credit where credit is due is important, but students should learn to cite sources for other reasons as well. The most important reason for citing sources is not to verify that students actually used sources or that they used the five sources required on the rubric. The most important reasons are to write with accuracy and to show students the importance of connecting their ideas to those of others or building upon them. The power of double-checking for accuracy ensures deeper learning as well. The infographic in Figure 4.4 summarizes the main ideas of read up, ask around, and double-check.[1]

WHAT IS FEEDBACK?

Defining *feedback* is easy, and so is recognizing it when it is encountered in many different forms. Essentially, *feedback* happens when a response to information from a source is sent back into the original system. Acoustic engineers systematically work to reduce and eliminate feedback. In the school auditorium, if the microphone is situated in a location where it picks up the sound from the speakers to which it is connected, the resulting screech you hear is feedback. The output from the speakers is fed back into the system through the microphone, complicating the signal and hurting the listeners' ears. The body of acoustic guitars can pick up and reamplify sounds, so musicians carefully select guitars crafted of wood that avoid the resulting extra information that detracts from the quality of the music.

A power company uses feedback about the amount of electricity consumed on a given day and orders more electricity to be generated as demand increases. The cruise control on your car uses feedback about speed and engine conditions to keep your speed constant, even when your car climbs a hill. In these cases, feedback is positive and useful. And your toddler daughter provides feedback to you if she slings her strained peas across the kitchen. Chances are good that you won't buy the strained peas again. Teachers often seek feedback about their teaching and provide feedback to their students about their performances. Like the screeching sound of the speakers or the monitors at the power company that tell engineers to increase the production of electricity, feedback is potentially useful, or it can be just a lot of noise. In this chapter, we explore feedback as a critical learning tool for the 21st-century teacher and student.

A common pattern in classrooms is the *teach–test–move on* paradigm. The instructor teaches, the students learn what they can, then the test is given at the end to document or certify how much each student has learned. Once the unit or lesson is completed, the class moves on, regardless of the success of the individual students on the test. Many would agree that this pattern is not ideal, but accountability mandates and the number of students in the class make it seem practical. This pattern is so ingrained in our society that it is difficult to conceptualize any other way of thinking about assessment. Study the drivers' handbook, take and pass the multiple-choice test, and you are licensed to drive.

---

[1] You can download a color version of this infographic for your classroom at *https://literacybeat.com/2019/03/26/read-up-ask-around-double-check*.

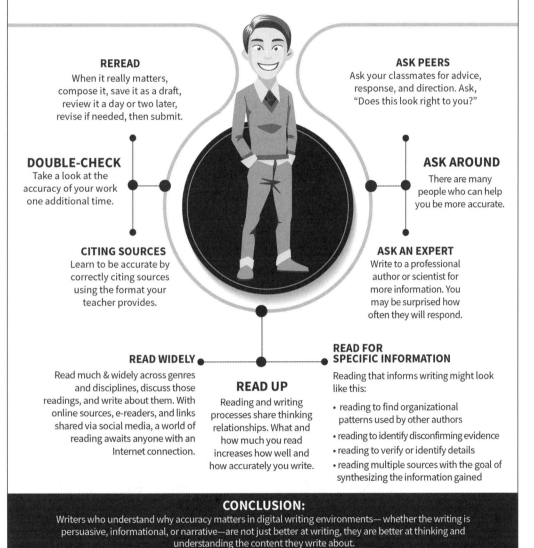

ACCURACY IN DIGITAL WRITING: READ UP, ASK AROUND, DOUBLE-CHECK

Here are some ways you can verify the authenticity of what you intend to convey in your work.

REREAD
When it really matters, compose it, save it as a draft, review it a day or two later, revise if needed, then submit.

ASK PEERS
Ask your classmates for advice, response, and direction. Ask, "Does this look right to you?"

DOUBLE-CHECK
Take a look at the accuracy of your work one additional time.

ASK AROUND
There are many people who can help you be more accurate.

CITING SOURCES
Learn to be accurate by correctly citing sources using the format your teacher provides.

ASK AN EXPERT
Write to a professional author or scientist for more information. You may be surprised how often they will respond.

READ WIDELY
Read much & widely across genres and disciplines, discuss those readings, and write about them. With online sources, e-readers, and links shared via social media, a world of reading awaits anyone with an Internet connection.

READ UP
Reading and writing processes share thinking relationships. What and how much you read increases how well and how accurately you write.

READ FOR SPECIFIC INFORMATION
Reading that informs writing might look like this:

• reading to find organizational patterns used by other authors
• reading to identify disconfirming evidence
• reading to verify or identify details
• reading multiple sources with the goal of synthesizing the information gained

CONCLUSION:
Writers who understand why accuracy matters in digital writing environments— whether the writing is persuasive, informational, or narrative—are not just better at writing, they are better at thinking and understanding the content they write about.

FIGURE 4.4. Infographic demonstrating read up, ask around, double-check.

However, assessment for student learning need not be a separate step apart from the instructional activities, and it need not produce anxiety for the learner. Assessment and instruction are complementary processes, and feedback is one of the bonds between them (see the classroom DNA model in Figure 3.2). Checking for understanding is the other bond, as we have seen. More important, useful feedback is the natural domain of the effective teacher, and it is quite common. One important purpose of this book, then, is to examine how to make feedback an integral and purposeful part of learning at school and to do so in a manner that is rigorous and precise.

Feedback, for instructional purposes, represents dynamic processes in which both teacher and student are actors. Feedback is interaction designed to promote learning, either between teacher and student or between students. It occurs in relation to a specific assignment or student-created artifact and instructional objectives.

Related to the idea of feedback is a well-known metaphor: scaffolding. Metaphors are useful because they highlight the relevant attributes of the target. A scaffold is a tool by which workers get at a part of a building that needs work but is not accessible without the tool (see Figure 4.5). Likewise, an instructional scaffold helps learners to understand what they otherwise could not if the scaffold weren't present. The end result in both cases is that the scaffold will no longer be needed, of course. The work on the building will be completed and the scaffolding removed; similarly, the learner will be able to accomplish the task or one similar to it without additional help. Popular tools, such as graphic organizers, are not scaffolds unless they have been employed in specific learning situations. More important, the tool

FIGURE 4.5. Djoser's pyramid in Egypt with construction scaffolds.

is not a scaffold unless it is needed by specific students to further their learning. Feedback becomes a scaffold if the information is somehow useful in achieving a new understanding that the learner can actually put to use.

Teaching with precision and reflective practice go hand in hand. Precision teaching means knowing how and when to release responsibility for learning gradually (Pearson & Gallagher, 1983). It means knowing our students and what they need in order to learn most effectively. It also means that we use just the right feedback to move student learning in a beneficial direction. When it comes to feedback, precision teaching also means recognizing areas to improve and acting consciously and deliberately to check that improvements occur (see also Fullan, Hill, & Crévola, 2006). Our working definition of what we mean when we refer to teaching with precision, informed by Fisher and colleagues (2016), is: "the value of matching specific instructional routines, procedures, or strategies with the appropriate phase of students' learning" (p. xii). In the next section, we explore how feedback, a critical teaching tool, can be done with precision.

ATTRIBUTES OF FEEDBACK

Figure 4.6 provides a typology of feedback attributes. As you read, look for these qualities in our examples and in your own practice. Four aspects of feedback help teachers think about what their own feedback might look like in the classroom. Hattie and Timperley (2007) suggest that feedback serves one of three purposes: *feed up, feed back,* and *feed forward.*

Feed up is goal related and tied to success criteria, including the level of challenge and the level of commitment to the goals. Feed up assists students in setting reasonable goals according to the feedback they have received. Commitment refers to the degree to which students will seek feedback in helping them shape their understanding of the goal, which may be a lesson objective or standard. It also refers to the degree to which teachers are willing to clearly align the goals and feed up to help students meet them. Models are a way teachers can help students understand the goals and provide them with a reference point for success. Feed up answers the question *Where am I, the student, going?*

Feed back, according to the Hattie and Timperley (2007) model, serves the purpose of assisting students to understand the process of how they are learning and accomplishing learning goals. Notice that *feed back* is two words, not one, to differentiate it from its one-word parent, *feedback.* Feed back provides students with information relative to the progress achieved, including useful benchmarks or checkpoints. To help students adjust gaps in their performance relative to progress, feed back answers the question *How am I going?*

Feed forward is information intended to help students to understand how they can improve self-regulation of their learning, and its nuances or complexities, and

Purposes	Types	Qualities	Forms
Feed back ("How am I going?") *Feed up* ("Where am I going?") *Feed forward* ("Where to next?")	Affirmations Clarifications Observations Corrections: content Corrections: mechanics, usage, spelling Questions Exploratory Personal	Identified positive aspects of the work Explains rather than labels Perceptive Corrective Compassionate Useful Timely Linked to specific criteria Expands, clarifies, elaborates Degree Notices and names	Written during Written after Oral during Oral after Teacher Peers Other parties Link to feed forward . . .

FIGURE 4.6. A typology of feedback.

aspire to greater challenges. Think of feed forward as feedback that opens additional possibilities for learning for students. Feed forward answers the student question *Where to next?*

Furthermore, teachers can direct feedback toward the task itself, the process or progress of the task, or the self-regulation of the task. As we have noted previously, feedback can also be directed toward the person or traits the student may appear to exhibit, but we have found that this type of feedback is not useful and is sometimes destructive to learning. Consider the following reading lesson with Ms. Smith-Corona and a small group of students.

Let's set the scene. When a student skips or substitutes a word while reading aloud, the teacher has several options, including ignoring the omission, supplying the missing word, supplying the missing word and asking the student to repeat it, asking the student to attend to phonetic cues, or asking the student to attend to context cues. What technique Ms. Smith-Corona chooses depends on what the reading goals for the lesson are: word recognition, decoding, fluency, and so on.

UNDERWOOD: (*reading aloud from Five Little Pigs [Kronheim, 1875]*[2]) This little

---

[2]Note: *Five Little Pigs* is a classic children's story reproduced online. Others are available at *https://americanliterature.com/short-stories-for-children.*

pig very much wanted to go with his brother, but as he was so miss . . . miss . . .

MS. SMITH-CORONA: Mischievous. Please repeat it. [Feed back]

UNDERWOOD: . . . mischievous that he could not be trusted far away. His mother made him stay at home and told him to keep a good fire while she went out to the millers to buy some flour.

[The students continue reading, and it is Olympia's turn.]

OLYMPIA: He had not gone far when he saw an old blind pig, who, with his hat in his hand, was crying at the loss of his pig.

MS. SMITH-CORONA: Remember our lesson when we talked about sentences that don't seem to make sense? Does this sentence make sense as you read it? [Feed up]

OLYMPIA: Oh, I see. He was crying at the loss of his dog!

MS. SMITH-CORONA: You got it! Okay, Remington, it is your turn to read.

REMINGTON: . . . so he put his hand in his pocket and found a *penny*, which he gave to the poor old pig. It was for such thoughtful conduct as this that his mother often gave this little pig roast beef.

MS. SMITH-CORONA: There is an unusual word, one we don't use very much these days in that sentence, Remington. Can you find it?

[Remington, Olympia, and Underwood put their fingers on the word *halfpenny* in their stories.]

MS. SMITH-CORONA: Right, we don't see that word very often, but you have seen the two parts of the word before. What do you think it says? [Feed forward]

REMINGTON: I think it is *half* and *penny* put together. *Halfpenny*?

MS. SMITH-CORONA: Let's keep reading.

In this reading interaction, Ms. Smith-Corona uses several types of feedback. She uses corrective feedback to help Underwood with the word *mischievous* that he tried but did not pronounce. Ms. Smith-Corona used a question to help Olympia realize her mistake and an affirmation to let her know she had corrected the error. Finally, the children explored a new skill, recognizing a compound word formed from a known word when Ms. Smith-Corona pointed out the error as Remington read aloud.

We have already explored several qualities of feedback in the preceding sections, and we continue doing so as we explore what precision feedback looks like.

STORIES FROM RESEARCH

Arlene Pincus, PhD, is a former elementary school principal and retired professor of literacy. She recognizes the value of feedback and the importance of students using that feedback to improve or shape their performances. The cumulative feedback table is a solution to the challenge teachers confront when their students may not see the value of the feedback available to them.

Using a Cumulative Feedback Table to Manage Individual- and Group-Writing Feedback

Arlene R. H. Pincus

What is more durable than a sticky note, has more clarity than handwriting, and is better organized than annotations in the margins? No doubt, all of them can come into play when providing writing feedback, and all involve a certain labor intensity that the *copy and paste* function of electronic text can overcome. Consider creating a cumulative feedback table (CFT) instead (see Figure 4.7 for an example).

A CFT can individualize feedback, encourage students' questions, track successes, and identify misunderstandings. It affords teachers and students some flexibility to add new goals and eliminate mastered ones. It can provide assessment data that are accessible to learners, their teachers, and other stakeholders in students' learning, such as parents and administrators.

When receiving the paper as electronic text, the teacher first reads the student's comments about the last paper (let's call that "Assignment 1"). The teacher then clears that space, reads the current paper (which we call "Assignment 2"), and adds comments about it, as shown in the left column of the figure. The teacher places the comments and highlighting within the paper that match the feedback contained in the checklist section of the CFT for the next assignment. The student reviews the teacher's comments about Assignment 1 and responds to the request to edit run-on sentences in the CFT (eliminating the need to return Assignment 1). The student then asks and answers any questions in the space provided (the figure's right column) in response to Assignment 2 and pastes the resulting CFT on top of Assignment 2.

Notice that the teacher has decided to offer a mini-lesson to several students about one writing idea, but has asked this particular student to consider editing the run-on sentences in the paper before offering individual instruction about this type of error. Class members would need to learn how to select the CFT when a paper is returned and copy it to the top of their subsequent papers. A typical student's personal CFT for one marking period or for a series of assignments is shown in Figure 4.7. A blank template of the CFT is available in Appendix E (see pp. 176–177).

Title of the Paper/Genre:	
Teacher's Comments and Questions about Paper 2: Student X, you can be proud of this paper for the following reasons: • We talked about how the beginning of a paper can draw your reader right in. When I read (first sentence is copied here), I really wanted to know more about _____. • I also noticed that your word choices were sophisticated and really helped me see what you were talking about. I highlighted some of these terrific choices (yellow). • You can see that you have made progress in almost every area we have discussed. • When we have our private conference, we can add other ideas and maybe take out some that we both think you have learned to make part of your writing. If you look at the places where I wrote an X for this week, you might have a go at revising these run-ons (highlighted in green) by following the directions in the box about how to edit each one. If you need assistance, we can talk about it. Look at the other places where you see an X for this week. Let's talk about them during Writing Workshop. I will invite a group of you to meet with me about this idea.	**Student's Comments and Questions:** *[They include the student's responses to the teacher's comments about the last paper, Paper 1. These comments are not shown here because this CFT shows what the teacher would return to the student with Paper 1.]*
Grade or rubric subgrades can go here:	

(continued)

FIGURE 4.7. Example of a cumulative feedback table for Assignment 2. Used by permission of Arlene R. H. Pincus.

Assignments (each number is a new assignment):	1	2	3	4	5	6	7	8	9
Purpose and audience:									
Is my lead compelling?	X	X	X						
Did I tell the reader what the reader needs to know?	X								
Does my ending work?	X	X							
Strong writing: (examples below)									
Descriptions: specific adjectives (examples: a *sizzling* meal, a *compelling* question)	X	X							
Strong Verbs: powerful verbs (examples: ? and ?)	X								
And so on . . . (lines can be added or deleted)									
Revising:									
Order of ideas. (example: student considers whether the information is given in a user-friendly order)	X								
Consider whether all of the ideas belong in this paper.		X		X					
And so on . . . (lines can be added or deleted)									
Editing:									
Please **use the spelling and grammar checker.**	X	X							
Check for run-on sentences (highlighted in green). Copy two of the three run-on sentences below and show how you would like to edit each.	X	X	X	X					

FIGURE 4.7. *(continued)*

PRECISION FEEDBACK

A few assumptions are in order here. Why? Often, what we humans take as truth is not exactly as advertised. Many teachers stop by the coffee pot in the staff room, and they believe that coffee is made from beans. Spoiler alert—they are not. What we call coffee beans are actually seeds. A bean contains seeds, but coffee is actually made from the seeds of the coffee plant. So, there's that. But what does this information have to do with feedback?

Perhaps we should try an assumption closer to home. Many students and parents believe that homework is universally a good idea. It is not in many cases (see Fisher et al., 2016). What about this one? Static-ability grouping addresses students' strengths and needs for improvement. *Hint:* It doesn't. Okay, but learning styles are verified science that informs instruction. Surely learning styles are a good idea. Nope. Such ideas are often appealing because they replicate a surface feature of our own experience (e.g., Pashler, McDaniel, Rohrer, & Bjork, 2008). We teachers want to believe that we have customized our instruction to the individual student, certainly a worthy goal. But what if our foundation for customizing that instruction has little or no effect on actual learning?

First, we need to challenge some assumptions about feedback. Try these out:

Praise is a good way to motivate students.

"Kudos!"; "Good job!"; "Well done!"; "Attaboy!" Who doesn't like to hear words of praise like these from time to time? Fine words indeed, but not helpful if we are trying to learn something new or redirect our efforts. Praise can feel very cuddly and warm, but how we use praise determines its effectiveness when we use praise as feedback. Other substitutes or proxies for "Nice work!" include rewards such as gold stars, bits of candy, and extra time at recess (e.g., Kohn, 1993).

In some cases, praise actually backfires. When a teacher says to a student, "You're so smart," it sounds like encouragement. The difficulty is that what students who hear such praise internalize is that their (perceived) character traits matter more than their performance (Mueller & Dweck, 1998). Traits, such as being smart, clever, and so on, are perceived by students and parents as fixed. They can't be changed, at least not easily. On the other hand, actions can be altered. Teachers who praise specific actions are more likely to affect results. Consider the difference between these types of praise:

TEACHER: Katie, you are such a good reader.

TEACHER: Katie, your use of voice inflections shows me that your reading fluency is improving.

Both are good things Katie would like to hear, but only the second one tells Katie exactly what she did that is notable. This type of specific praise highlights good performance. Sometimes students don't know exactly what they did well, and praise helps them know what efforts pay off.

 Wise teacher tip: All the effective teachers we know handle praise this way, but we can all use a reminder from time to time. Specific, positive praise in public is useful, but corrective praise should be done as quietly and anonymously as possible. In Katie's case, telling her that reading fluently with inflection also reverberates around the reading group if she is given this feedback when others can hear it. They will note what Katie did, and that it is perhaps one way to improve their own performances. The ripple effect of positive and precise praise can be astounding.

There is an unintended consequence to some types of feedback that might be viewed as the opposite of praise but are given with kindness. Most teachers have heard a parent say something along these lines: "I know Andrey isn't very good at spelling, but then I wasn't either when I was in school." You can insert any number of subjects instead of spelling: history, math, writing, and so on. The intent of the sentiment is kindness in the face of difficulty, but the effect is very different. The message that "not everyone can be good at spelling" becomes internalized as a trait that can't be changed (Rattan, Good, & Dweck, 2012). The script that runs in the student's mind is, "If I am not good at spelling, I might as well get used to it. Why try?"

Praising actions, not traits (see Hattie & Timperley, 2007), is a mindset that the most effective teachers we know rely on as a way to indicate to students that they are in control of their learning. Moreover, it suggests the possibility of success. Learning to praise actions and not traits takes practice.

 Sage leader tip: Teachers are busy people. You already knew that, but you can help. Just as our students sometimes need help remembering what a good performance looks like, teachers do, too. A good use of time in the faculty meeting may include practice in offering effective praise. Have a teacher role-play being the student who has just done something well, while the other partner takes on the teacher role and praises the action. It may seem a little silly at first, but practice makes perfect. Now, where have we heard that before?

Thanks!

TEACHER: Olga, would you pick up that piece of paper on the floor?

OLGA: (*Picks up the paper and throws it in the trash can.*)

TEACHER: Thank you, Olga.

Sounds like praise, doesn't it? Acknowledging expected behaviors are not the same thing as praising them in students' minds, though. Sometimes we just reinforce or acknowledge behaviors that we expect but are sometimes forgotten. We expect students to pick up trash and throw it away, but sometimes they may not see the trash, or they may think picking up the garbage is someone else's responsibility.

At other times, teachers can reinforce expected behaviors so that they become routine—for example, "Oscar, I see you have begun writing your essay. Nice! But, please remember to put your name on the paper in the upper right corner first." We expect Oscar to write his name on his paper, but for whatever reason, today he forgot to do it. By making the request and then acknowledging his response, we reinforce that behavior for the future. There is no point, in our experience, in becoming exasperated that Oscar has once again forgotten to put his name on his paper. Making a big deal of it ("Oscar, how many times have I told you?") only deflects Oscar from writing his essay with his name on the paper. Acknowledging what is expected, just by saying "thank you," is a form of feedback that reinforces expected behaviors and performances.

Students don't know what they don't know.

The problem here is that sometimes they do know what the problem might be. As Freire (1993) pointed out, learners are not blank slates just waiting for someone to uncork the bottle and pour the knowledge into their heads. Sometimes, learners are already aware of the problem, or at least that there might be a problem. Sometimes, learners, even adults in a work environment, know that there is a problem and that they have the necessary knowledge; they just don't know how to put that knowledge into action (Zenger & Folkman, 2016). When corrective or positive feedback is offered safely, learners are more likely to understand and even want corrective feedback that helps them improve their performance.

Safe environments actually encourage taking risks, a trait that scholars and entrepreneurs value around the globe. Fred Keil, a noted expert on chief executive officer (CEO) effectiveness, points out, "Virtuoso CEOs were all highly self-aware. They had a long history of seeking feedback. They made it safe for people to give them feedback and tell them the truth" (Moosath, 2015, p. 79). If teachers are the CEOs of their classrooms (that is, chief education officers), they must model the very behaviors they expect of students. Students who accept feedback and use it as a critical component of their learning are often in the classes taught by teachers who have long sought feedback from principals, coaches, mentors, and other students and incorporate it in their practice. Corrective feedback that includes a dire consequence probably does not provide a safe place for students to take the necessary risks that lead to better learning.

My students should "know" this.

Curriculum maps, textbooks, and standards may give the appearance that learning is a linear process and that knowledge is acquired one building block at a time. However, this model of learning and cognition doesn't always reflect the way humans acquire and use knowledge. We know that learning to read can be facilitated by teaching some aspects of phonics in a specific order (e.g., Ehri, 1994). But learning is also highly dependent on variables, such as local conditions and contexts. Experiences and current skills and competencies affect what we and our students learn. Sometimes, students' attention is misdirected (and here we mean that the students were paying attention, but not to what we planned). Teachers experience the same issues. We and our colleagues (Young et al., 2017) found that what new or novice teachers can apply from a teacher preparation program is highly dependent on the expectations and support they receive in their initial teaching assignments after they leave the program. No matter how much we attempt to impose a structure on learning, much of what we learn is idiosyncratic, too.

A few years ago, one of us (Thomas) went on a sailing adventure aboard the replica Coast Guard revenue cutter, *Californian*. Sixteen students, a science teacher, and I left port under the ship's expert crew headed for Anacapa Island off the coast of California (see Figure 4.8). Students took turns at the helm, but they steered to the left, a little right, a quick overcorrection left, and so on. When it was my turn

FIGURE 4.8. The *Californian* in San Diego harbor.

at the helm, they noticed that there were no big swings port to starboard and back. One quick young man asked me, "How come when you steer we stay on course?"

While the students were at the helm, they looked at the binnacle (the compass) and made big corrections, without accounting for wind and current. They looked at the bow and made corrections accordingly. These young sailors had never been at sea before, so they followed their instincts, paying attention to what seemed the reasonable sources of information at the front of the ship. What did they need to do in this teachable moment? They needed to quit looking at the compass and the bow so often, and start looking in the direction they were heading, keeping their eyes on the destination, while only occasionally looking at the compass. In this case, the student sailors had the right idea (keep on course), but they didn't know where their attention needed to be. They found that they could steer a much truer course just by looking ahead beyond the bow of the ship. That night, not even Hollywood and all the special effects in a movie studio arsenal could recreate the feeling of wind in the sails, stars overhead, and students who had learned where their attention would be most effective.

Feedback, whenever.

Do you ever feel like we do sometimes? We have 200 students and only 24 hours in the day, but we still try to return students' assignments as fast as we can. Thank goodness for weekends! Timeliness matters. We return to this topic in Box 4.2 at the end of this chapter, where parents Miral El Deeb and Passant Mahmoud describe their experiences.

CRITICAL FEEDBACK

When each of us—Susan, Dana, and Thomas—were classroom teachers early in our careers, we assigned students to write, and they did. We collected their work and took it home to score over the weekend. Our young writers were clever and creative, but as inexperienced writers they needed our help. We tossed our red pens aside and used green or purple ink to make the feedback look friendlier, and we marked every error and wrote many comments for improvement. Of course, a grade was always included on the last page in the hope that students would read the feedback provided before looking at the grade. They didn't. Instead, they flipped right to the last page, noted the grade, and that was it. The paper was jammed to the bottom of the backpack, never to see the light of day again. We each concluded that something needed to change.

The idea behind giving feedback is that students should act on the information provided, or at least give it due consideration. Even though experiences like ours, which we've just described, seem to show that students do not want feedback, especially if it is critical, our experience suggests otherwise. Students need time built in to the structure of assignments so that they can act on the feedback provided. And, of course, they need feedback that is just right.

For surface-level grammatical and spelling errors, it can be helpful to provide a minimal amount of feedback. Hyland (1990) and others have noted that indirect, rather than direct, feedback is often more effective. Other research shows that there are marginal, positive effects for direct feedback on English as a foreign language (EFL) students' writing (Karim & Nassaji, 2018). A look at direct and indirect feedback reveals some of the nitty gritty of providing precise feedback.

In direct feedback, the teacher marks the error and provides the correction. For example:

ate
Yesterday, a camel ~~eated~~ a man's hat near the pyramids at Giza.

Indirect feedback can take a couple of different forms. In this example, the teacher has identified the error and indicated what type of problem is presented. It is up to the student to figure out how to correct the error.

irregular verb
Yesterday, a camel <u>eated</u> a man's hat near the pyramids at Giza.

Even less information is provided in this example of indirect feedback, with only the error being identified with a check in the margin.

☑ Yesterday, a camel eated a man's hat near the pyramids at Giza.

Hyland (1990) suggests that indirect feedback is less useful when students are working with challenging ideas than it is when corrections are surface-level errors. The precision needed has to be determined by a teacher who has taught well, such that students can make use of the feedback no matter how direct or indirect it is. And, of course, different students may need differing levels of feedback support.

It may stand to reason that people, students included, prefer positive or reinforcing feedback over negative, corrective, or redirecting feedback. A study by Zenger and Folkman (2014), reported in the *Harvard Business Review,* asked employees from various international settings about their feedback preferences. One surprising finding was that employees actually want corrective or redirecting feedback because it helps them perform well in their jobs. Perhaps that is a function of the relationship quality between the recipient of the feedback and the person providing it. We return to that notion in the next section.

Although knowing what type of feedback to provide and what purpose it serves is important, the degree, or amount, of nudging, praise, or redirection we give is equally important. Just as students often know that something is wrong, precision feedback suggests that adjusting how much, or to what degree, we provide feedback is a critical factor.

When we give feedback to our students, sometimes we couch our comments in terms of strengths and weaknesses. Okay, fair enough. The teacher's job is to help students to be the best they can at any given time and to realize that there are incorrect ways to do things. We never say anymore that there are "no wrong answers." Very often, we quickly discover that there are. However, depending on the question or prompt, we can say that there are "many right answers." Our choice of words points students in the direction we want them to go. In the same vein, we try to avoid using the phrase *strengths and weaknesses* and instead talk about *strengths and challenges*. Why? Now, that's a good question.

 Magician tip: Screencasting is a technique that employs software that captures what is on the screen while the screencaster narrates. For teachers, screencasting can be a time-saver because a students' essay or digital artifact can be displayed on the screen as the teacher provides feedback on specific attributes of the students' work. The recording is saved, and the teacher can then send students a link to the file for them to review.

Because I said so.

When the fourth student asks for the fifth time why she must do something, it is tempting to say, "Because I told you to do it." How teachers deploy authority in the classroom is vitally critical to the quality of the feedback they provide. Some of the reasons for this are obvious, but others are more deeply rooted in how we educators approach the task of guiding our students toward excellence.

First, we posit that the relationship between the teacher and his students is paramount, and that effective feedback can be a catalyst for improved relationships. Students might comply with a teacher who relies on the authority granted by the school to teach, but learning and continually improving their knowledge and learning abilities depend more on whether the students trust the teacher to promote what they do well and help them see their own versions of excellence.

Second, precision feedback is possibly rooted better in knowing when a student has done something well rather than when a task or performance is less than optimal. Buckingham and Goodall (2019) lead research into productivity at the ADP Research Institute and Cisco Systems, respectively. They push back against the idea that any one person is a fount of excellence that can be conveyed to any employee or student willing to listen and take to heart the feedback provided. Research into evaluative feedback, they suggest, shows that often more than 50% of the feedback provided is reflective of the person giving the feedback and his or her idiosyncratic understandings of abstract notions of excellence. To illustrate, they cite the excellent work of comedians, who all approach the task of making people laugh in completely different ways, and of athletes, who often accomplish the same outcome of scoring points using many different techniques. No set criterion for humor or for scoring free-throw points will create excellence in these endeavors. We believe that this principle applies in our classrooms, too.

Because human brains are wired as they are, focusing on our strengths results in dense areas of neuronal connections. By directing attention to a person's strengths, the possibility of learning is greatly increased, in part because the fight-or-flight response in the brain is not activated. Teachers who are able to identify what students do well and help them understand that they have, in fact, done something well are more likely to inspire excellent work. By contrast, criticism or focusing on shortcomings triggers the fight-or-flight response, and learning is impaired as a result.

So, what does this mean for us as teachers? When we provide feedback, we must first realize that much of our feedback reflects our own personalities and our understanding of what we teach, and not an entirely objective view of what constitutes a good performance. It is for this reason that relationships between students and teachers are the lynchpin to precision feedback. Humility that recognizes that who we are as teachers can have positive or less happy consequences for our students. Students who do not trust the teacher to recognize their strengths or to demonstrate competence in the subject area are less likely to learn in that classroom.

The art of using strengths to achieve success is about fostering the students' capacities to identify their successes and construct, bit by bit, nuanced understandings, creative riffs on what they know, and necessary improvements they can pursue on their own. Here, our own experience as well as that of researchers in business, neuroscience, and psychology suggest that feedback is far more complicated, if it is to be effective, than simply pointing out what is incorrect, what a shortcoming or deficit might be, or what to do next to meet or exceed this or that standard.

THE RIGHT WORDS

Classroom relationships often depend on the words teachers and students choose to communicate what is important and where our attention should be focused and how members of a civil society conduct themselves. Buckingham and Goodall (2019) believe that we can only bring our own perceptions and experiences to the feedback interaction. They suggest that feedback be given based on this premise. For example, instead of saying to a student, "You need to focus on your communication skills," the teacher can say, "Here is exactly where you lost me during your presentation." Instead of "You should do this next," try "Here is what I would try next." You can see how the focus of the first statement is on a perceived deficit exhibited by the student, the "you" in the message. The focus of the second statement builds on the trust the teacher engenders in her students, the idea that "I," the teacher you trust, has an idea you might find useful. In this way, the teacher allows the student to make choices that depend on his or her strengths.

Teachers, according to Johnston (2004), can catalyze learning through several different moves they can make in discourse with their students. He points out that how we use language in the classroom changes the nature of the influence we have as to whether students will accept our feedback and as to the extent they trust that feedback. Noticing what students have accomplished and pointing that out to them is one way. "Wendy, did you see what you did there? You spelled the word *conscience* correctly. Many people miss this one and spell it as *conscious*." Another way is to name something successful a student has done:

> TEACHER: Youssef, I see here in your story that you have a reference to a fire out of control, and later your main character is caught in a house fire.
>
> YOUSSEF: Right, I was giving the reader some notice of how things might go.
>
> TEACHER: Excellent, we call that technique "foreshadowing," and it is something experienced novelists do often.

What do you suppose the likelihood is that Youssef will attempt foreshadowing an event in a future story will be? We think it's very likely now that he knows what it is he did well and what it is called.

Johnston (2004) also suggests that teachers use a discourse move that helps point students in the direction they might take in responding to each other and to the teacher. A teacher might ask, "What did you learn today as a reader?" gently pointing the student to her strengths as a reader. "As writers, what do you think we can do to solve this problem with the plot?"

TACTICAL AND STRATEGIC FEEDBACK (ON THE SPOT AND PLANNED)

Feedback is often planned. It can also be strategic when you plan to read students drafts and guide them with specific feedback relative to the writing goals. There is a section in Appendix B (pp. 170–171) where you can describe any planned feedback. The same is true when you plan to have your students use the rubric or other grading criteria to provide feedback to each other, as they would in a writing workshop (e.g., Atwell, 1987). At other times, the feedback you or others (such as other students in the classroom) provide is tactical. It occurs in the moment when complications, unforeseen circumstances, or misinterpretations arise. It comes into play when teachers foresee that as students' assessment stories evolve, there will be challenges, opportunities, and difficulties that occur anytime humans are involved in a learning enterprise.

Finally, we emphasize that teachers are not the only source of useful feedback. Parents, other students, siblings, friends, and other teachers or mentors all offer sources of useful feedback. In a study of refugee students in Lebanon (Karkouti, Toprak, & Wolsey, 2019), students often turned to their older siblings, family, and friends to learn more about their performance in school.

STORIES FROM PARENTS

Miral and Passant are parents of students enrolled at schools in Cairo, Egypt. International schools in Egypt often emulate, or base, their mission and curriculum on models from other countries, such as the American, Finnish, and British models, and so on. National (public) schools feature a very traditional approach to education that does not emphasize the role of feedback and teacher–student relationships. Because teachers in the national system are poorly paid, they often seek additional compensation by tutoring students privately (see Wolsey, in press). Their perspective offers us an opportunity to view how parents perceive assessment and feedback.

Classroom Assessment and Feedback from the Parents' Point of View

MIRAL EL DEEB AND PASSANT HESHAM MAHMOUD

Classroom assessment is an integral part of education that is applied similarly as a concept in most educational institutes, but assessment methods can be different from one place to another. The purpose of assessment has also changed from being merely a way of determining the amount of learning the students have acquired to a much broader and vital purpose (Manitoba Education, Citizenship, and Youth [MECY], 2006). In addition, assessment methods are now evaluated for quality assurance in terms of reliability, validity, and reference points. Classroom assessment can be viewed as a process that starts with gathering information, interpreting information, continues with record keeping, and ends with communicating results. In each of these four steps, the teacher has a particular role and has to make certain decisions regarding what to assess and which methods of assessment to use that ensure quality and fairness (MECY, 2006). As much as the information that teachers gather using assessment methods is important, how they will proceed further with this information is what really matters. This is the part of the assessment process in which communication or feedback takes place. Feedback involves students; school administrators such as supervisors, department heads, and principals; and parents. Feedback to students can be given in so many ways and with various techniques, some of which can be effective and successful and some that are not. Reflecting on our own personal experiences, as two mothers with children enrolled in primary-level classes in Egyptian schools, we have come face-to-face with some of the successful feedback techniques and were unfortunate enough to encounter some others that failed to yield positive results.

Our own struggle with current feedback techniques in Egyptian schools triggered the research done for this essay in an attempt to gather more information about teacher–student feedback and how it can be properly and most effectively conveyed. Does one-to-one teacher–student feedback actually take place in schools? Is teacher–student feedback in Egyptian schools similar to that in other schools worldwide?

Recent studies have put more emphasis on assessment feedback as a major part of the student learning process (Heritage, 2011). Assessment feedback recommended by scholars and researchers proved to have a great impact on pushing student learning forward during its development phase. A commonly cited definition of formative feedback states that it is "information about the gap between the actual level and reference level which is used to alter that gap" (Ramaprasad, 1983, p. 4). Nowadays, feedback studies are taking a slightly different approach toward assessment feedback practices. Instead of the teacher simply informing the student about how to improve, studies emphasize that involving the student in the feedback process is more effective and efficient. There should be a two-way communication channel between the teacher and student. In addition, the teacher should tailor his or her feedback style to match the needs of every student.

DISCUSSIONS ON ACTUAL APPLICATIONS IN EGYPT

In shedding light on the application of assessment feedback in governmental (public) schools in Egypt, one realizes that in most cases, there is a huge gap between literature on the subject and reality. Unfortunately, there are almost no published resources regarding the application of feedback in Egyptian public schools to which we could refer. Most of the information gathered in this section is from personal communication with teachers or parents from our children's schools.

Focusing on feedback related to formative writing assignments, some teachers just provide a grade, applying the traditional one-way feedback system discussed earlier. They regard their grading as sufficient feedback and maintain that students should understand by themselves what is required to improve their grades. "Historically, teachers had corrected student work without any theory of feedback being involved. Marking was regarded as a process intrinsic to teaching" (Boud & Molloy, 2013, p. 700). A limited number of public schools in Egypt require the teachers to write down notes for the students, in which they are given instructions or guidelines to improve their writing skills.

On the other hand, a study conducted by Dr. Abdel Salam El Koumy (2009) at Menouf Secondary School for Boys showed also that students at the secondary level are weak in basic and inferential reading in English. The reason is that the teachers spend most of their time on preparing their students for high-stakes tests. Their main goal is to help the students learn how to answer comprehension questions or to guess the answer when they do not know the correct one. The teachers also spend a long time familiarizing the students with exam strategies, rather than allocating time to teaching them reading comprehension (El Koumy, 2009). The students lack reading strategies and focus on memorization. Still, exam grades are the most important and main concern of students, teachers, and parents. Since students are not examined in reading skills, the skills are marginalized and neglected. The teachers at Menouf Secondary School do not assign any time to feedback. However, it is worth mentioning that the study conducted by El Koumy demonstrated that when the students were provided with the *feed-back* and *feed-forward* techniques, there was an improvement in reading and in exam grades.

In talking with teachers regarding the reasons behind not spending enough time on feedback, the common reason we generally discovered were that "time does not allow it." Other factors that were given for not giving feedback include:

1. The curriculum is intensive, and teachers do not have time to waste on student conferences.
2. Feedback is not regarded as a beneficial tool for learning or as a means of instruction.
3. Teachers do not get extra pay if they spend more time with students to work on their weaknesses. They assume that students will improve their writing skills by doing more reading and writing.
4. Teachers do not receive any professional development, such as workshops or training, to learn how to provide effective feedback.

Furthermore, communicating informally with some parents and students revealed to us that they do not understand the importance of feedback as well. They regard "explaining lessons" as the most important function of the teacher and believe that assessments just show whether students understood the assigned curriculum or not. They also see no difference between formative and summative assessments and consider both types as methods of testing.

CONCLUSION AND RECOMMENDATIONS

After looking at the work of many scholars who tackled the concept of feedback and learning, it can be inferred that there is a huge gap between feedback as described in recent research and feedback that is practically applied by teachers in Egyptian schools. Even though feedback applications have significantly developed over the past few years, a lot of schools still fail to properly implement feedback techniques, leading to some overlooked learning opportunities for students. There are several factors that could be responsible, such as the lack of knowledge and models teachers have on feedback, the shortage in training given to teachers on feedback, misconceptions or incorrect perceptions that teachers have about feedback, and the time constraints in implementing feedback.

Most schools and teachers focus on the curriculum, the teaching methods, and the lesson plans and fail to give feedback the same attention. In the majority of schools, especially here in Egypt, student feedback is limited to only grading and teacher–parent conferences. If feedback sometimes takes place, it is usually informal and not well constructed or planned. Public schools in Egypt and Egyptian culture place a high value on grades and results, and the majority of parents themselves care most about final grades.

The knowledge teachers have about feedback is very limited and does not reflect the main purpose behind effective feedback. The characteristics of effective feedback have been tackled by several scholars. According to Wiggins (2012), there are seven keys to effective feedback. It should be goal referenced, tangible and transparent, actionable, user-friendly, timely, ongoing, and consistent. Moreover, rarely do teachers receive specialized training on feedback, which means they never fully learn about its value in the learning journey. Feedback in the form of letter grades and numbers still prevails in schools, without the need for any further explanation to the student receiving these grades. If teachers learn more about the different types of feedback and how they can be effective when used appropriately, they will devote more effort to guiding their students through feedback to help them reach their learning potential. Also, teachers still have misconceptions about feedback; they still see it as only the result of a certain lesson, task, or assignment. They fail to see it as an opportunity for students to learn from their mistakes and make improvements. They insist on seeing it as the end and not the means to an end. Some even view feedback as a reward or punishment for a student's performance and use it to make judgments on a student's academic level, instead of viewing feedback as a learning opportunity and a chance for students to learn more and expand their knowledge.

Unfortunately, though, applying effective feedback can be very time-consuming and might not be welcomed by many teachers and schools. This is specifically relevant for one-to-one verbal or written feedback between the teacher and the student. At this point, schools who wish to apply proper feedback to enhance the quality of student learning need to make detailed plans and decisions according to their priorities as educators.

Considering these difficulties, we offer a few recommendations to help improve the quality of feedback implemented in schools, such as:

- Feedback offered to students must be specific and planned in advance and not vaguely and haphazardly given.

- Feedback must be high quality, timely, accurate, constructive, outcome focused, encouraging, and positive.

- Feedback should focus on what the student did correctly and what needs to be done to improve future performance.

To fulfill the above objectives, the following points need to be taken into consideration:

- A well-defined professional development plan is needed in order for teachers to change their perception of feedback and their current practices. There are several plans available online that could be used. For example, one of the online articles is a comprehensive workshop study conducted by Fonseca and colleagues (2015) that aims to change teachers' feedback practices with a prepared and detailed action plan. The workshop is divided into five sessions focusing on feedback strategies, such as time (immediate or delayed), audience (one-to-one or group), mode (oral or written), and content (detailed or general). In addition, the workshop also includes the teacher's tone and communication skills. Teachers should attend similar workshops to improve their feedback practices and skills.

- Teachers should recognize that feedback is a type of instructional method, as it helps students recognize their status and learn how to reach their target (i.e., how to assess their strengths and work on areas of challenge). The simile we constructed to further explain this is that teachers should visualize themselves as coaches on a playing field who have the means of directing the players to the targeted goal, as well as motivate and inspire them to play better and excel. Furthermore, by collecting evidence during the game (i.e., "the class assessment"), the teacher can adjust his or her teaching techniques to meet the students' present learning levels.

- Students, as well as teachers, need to be aware of the benefits of feedback. Sadler (2013) also emphasized the importance of including the two parties, both teacher and student, in the feedback process. Teachers can play a crucial role in providing students with tools, such as rubrics or checklists, that can assist them in improving their performance.

- Teachers should also collaborate together to improve feedback practices.

- School leaders need to give priority to feedback and encourage teachers to exert more effort and spend more time with students to give them effective feedback.

- School leaders can also conduct "awareness sessions" for students and parents to learn the importance of feedback and alter their perceptions about it. Schools could hold orientation sessions for students and parents, in which they explain the importance of feedback and its impact on the learner's journey. They should believe that it will benefit the students and mainly aim to move them forward.

- In addition, students need to understand that their assessment feedback is confidential and will not be disclosed to their classmates. Therefore, teachers should pay attention to how students are perceiving their feedback. Many of them perceive feedback as unhelpful and do not make any use of it in their future work, despite the effort consumed in the process (Sadler, 2013). Such students might change their perception if they are involved in the assessment feedback process. They need to be aware of their learning goals and monitor themselves through the learning process (Andrews, Brown, & Mesher, 2018).

CHAPTER 5

Artifacts and Tools for Assessment

Sometimes it is difficult to separate the assessment instrument from the assessment itself. Throughout this book, we work toward a definition of assessment that focuses on the stories that assessment tells. The most important story to be told, of course, is that of the individual students. Perhaps it is too nitpicky of us to say that a test is *not* an assessment, but what the teacher learns from the test results *is* an assessment. However, this idea helps us highlight our purpose in writing this book—and your purpose in reading it and, hopefully, applying its ideas. It is sometimes too easy, too tempting to mistake the map for the territory (Korzybski, 1933; Wolsey, 2006) and to think of the test as the actual learning it is meant to represent.

WHAT DO WE MEAN BY *ASSESSMENT TOOLS?*

Teachers use many tools and artifacts to assess student learning, understanding, and behavior in the classroom. Students' behaviors, their assignments, and their interactions all provide information that teachers may use to determine how well students are learning. So in assessing learning, we use a variety of tools and artifacts. A *tool*, for our purposes here, is an instrument or product that is used to teach and to assess our teaching and students' learning. For example, many teachers use concept maps or graphic organizers during instruction. The point of asking students to use a concept map is not to check whether students can complete a concept map. Rather, the point is to help students visually display their knowledge and perhaps construct knowledge of their understanding (Lapp, Wolsey, & Wood, 2015). Thus, the concept map is a tool that helps teachers assess students' understanding, at the same time that students use it to develop that understanding. Rubrics, which we discuss later in the chapter, are another example of an assessment tool.

An *artifact* is a student work product that can be assessed for information about student learning. An argumentative essay that a student has written is an artifact that provides information within a framework, such as standards, lesson objectives, and expectations for writing. We include several examples, which you should feel free to adapt, in the Assessing the Assessments instruments in the appendices.

An exit ticket (see Chapter 4) is another example of an artifact. If a teacher provides a written prompt for what to write (see Figure 4.2 on p. 52 for types of exit tickets), the prompt is a tool.

Processes that don't produce visual evidence may also be used to assess. Teachers who ask questions, as we described in Chapter 3, are assessing their students' understanding. Through good questioning, the teacher improves student learning by prodding for higher-order thinking or by nudging students to notice some aspect of a concept they had not yet noticed. Here we take a look at some of the more frequently used tools, artifacts, and assessment processes.

Questions: A Time-Honored Tradition

Over three decades ago, Daines (1986) published a study showing that 38 teachers in grades 2 through 12 employed four types of questions in their classrooms: literal, interpretive, application, and affective. Interpretive questions required students to make inferences, compare or contrast, determine cause-and-effect relationships, make predictions based on trends, and so on. Based on observation and analysis of the teachers' lessons, 93% of the 5,289 questions teachers asked during this study were at the literal level. Less than 7% were interpretive questions. Teachers asked about 78 questions per hour, and second-grade teachers asked the most questions. Tenth-grade teachers asked the fewest questions. On average, teachers only waited 2 seconds from the time the question was asked until a student responded, and this time did not increase when higher-order questions were asked. You are probably wondering how long the average student's response was. It was only 3 seconds, with a range that extended to 5 seconds in 10th grade.

In Turkey, Seker and Kömür (2008) found that students in teacher preparation programs for English language teaching who did not exhibit critical thinking in an essay exercise also did not ask higher-order questions (see Bloom's revised taxonomy in Anderson and Krathwohl, 2001) when they were teaching. These researchers suggested the need for greater attention to questioning skills as teachers-to-be prepare for their first teaching jobs.

The research points out just what we might expect: Teachers asked higher-order questions when they planned those questions in advance, allowing for flexibility as a discussion evolves. Literal-level questions do have a place, but as a kind of default when questions are not thoughtfully prepared before a teacher-led discussion. Teachers can provide opportunities for students to think through their responses in several ways:

- Increasing the wait time between asking a question and expecting students to respond.
- Asking students to write tentative responses in a journal or in their notes before being asked to respond.
- Allowing students to work out responses in small groups or pairs.

Sometimes students require extra assistance in formulating their responses. They may know the content, but knowing the answer and being able to provide the answer are not necessarily the same thing. A bit of scaffolding can help students respond to higher-level thinking. Sentence frames put the priority on the response by providing a framework that students can use to get started and experiment with academic language at the same time.

Diane Lapp and her colleague Amy Miles developed an organizer with language frames in Figure 5.1 to help students analyze an argument they encounter in an article they were given to read. By writing down the elements of the argument (or noting the lack of an argument), students start to acquire the skills necessary to recognize thoughtful arguments and construct their own. They ask students to use Educreations (*www.educreations.com*) to record their critique of the article and then share it with their classmates.

Building on the practicality of using sentence frames, Lapp and Miles constructed the bookmark (shown in Figure 5.2 on p. 84) for their students to use.

Discussion and Collaboration

Discussion as a means of creating meaning is as old as Socrates. Assessing discussion is another problem entirely. What should a teacher do? Count the number of times a student participates orally? That's a quagmire because sometimes the student who talks the most contributes the least, and sometimes the student who contributes once or twice has been thoughtfully considering the ideas of all her peers before saying that one pithy comment that is right on point. One difficulty with assessing a discussion among students and the quality of their participation is that it is time intensive for the teacher, or whoever is doing the assessing.

Assessing participation in a whole-class discussion is a challenge for the teacher who is attempting to engage students' interest, but it is even more difficult when students work in small groups. Arguably, small groups offer greater interaction among participants, but from an assessment standpoint the teacher can only collect a few snapshots by listening in before moving on to the next group. A solution to this problem may be found in self-assessment (Docan-Morgan, 2015).

Examine the student essay at your table. The essay is missing the coding for the claim, evidence, warrant, and counterclaim. Take a picture or scan of the essay and, using Educreations, record a critique. Use the following sentence starters and chart to plan what you will say and underline in your recording.

	Possible Language Frames	Which sentence will you underline/highlight?
Claim (underline)	In this essay the writer is making the claim that _____. I can tell because _____.	
Evidence (circle)	The evidence used to support the claim is _____ _____. The writer uses language like _____ that lets me know it is evidence. Additional evidence is _____ that lets me know that _____.	
Warrant (square)	The warrant for this evidence is _____ _____, and it supports the claim because _____. Another warrant is _____ and supports the claim because _____.	
Counterclaim (squiggly underline)	The counterclaim is _____. The writer uses words like _____. Another counterclaim is _____.	
Additional comments you could say	This person forgot to add the _____. One thing that is incomplete is _____. I like how this essay _____. I agree with this person's claim that _____ because _____.	

FIGURE 5.1. Argumentative critique planning guide. From Wolsey and Lapp (2017). Copyright © 2017 The Guilford Press. Reprinted with permission.

From Wolsey and Lapp (2017). Copyright © 2017 The Guilford Press. Reprinted by permission in *Assessment Literacy: An Educator's Guide to Understanding Assessment, K–12,* by Thomas DeVere Wolsey, Susan Lenski, and Dana L. Grisham (The Guilford Press, 2020). Permission to photocopy this figure is granted to purchasers of this book for personal use or use with students (see copyright page for details). Purchasers can download enlarged versions of this figure (see box at the end of the table of contents).

CLAIM	I will argue that _____ _____. This paper will show that _____ _____.
EVIDENCE	One piece of evidence is _____ _____. Another piece of evidence to support my claim is _____ _____. Additional evidence is _____ _____. To support the claim that _____, _____.
WARRANT	As a rule, _____ _____. Generally speaking, _____ _____. Most people would agree that _____ _____. It is the accepted belief that _____ _____. Some may argue that _____ _____. The truth is _____ _____.
COUNTERCLAIM AND COUNTER TO COUNTERCLAIM	There are those who would claim _____ _____, however, _____. Some people think _____ _____. But in reality, _____ _____. It is possible to argue that _____ _____. Upon closer inspection, however, ____ _____.

FIGURE 5.2. Sentence frames to support crafting an argument. From Wolsey and Lapp (2017). Copyright © 2017 The Guilford Press. Reprinted with permission.

From Wolsey and Lapp (2017). Copyright © 2017 The Guilford Press. Reprinted by permission in *Assessment Literacy: An Educator's Guide to Understanding Assessment, K–12*, by Thomas DeVere Wolsey, Susan Lenski, and Dana L. Grisham (The Guilford Press, 2020). Permission to photocopy this figure is granted to purchasers of this book for personal use or use with students (see copyright page for details). Purchasers can download enlarged versions of this figure (see box at the end of the table of contents).

Participation logs are easily adaptable and require students to think through their participation as defined by the teacher over time. In the example in Figure 5.3, students were asked to log their participation during the week (or month or semester) and report their reflections. Participation logs the students create are a tool that helps the teacher determine what students contribute, while simultaneously encouraging them to do so.

An advantage of participation logs is that students can also share their perceptions of the instruction or points of confusion. These log entries can also guide the teacher who needs feedback from the students. How might you use participation logs in a learning management system (such as, Blackboard, Canvas, or Moodle) or via Twitter or another student-response system?

Observation

Perhaps one of the most powerful classroom assessment tools is *observation*. Yetta Goodman (1985) coined the term *kid watching,* or purposeful observations of students. Teachers can learn a great deal about the children in their classrooms just by being observant. Because it is difficult to watch every student every minute, we have instead focused on three or four specific students each day. We ask ourselves how the students react to instruction and reflect on our interactions with those students. Our colleagues can help us with this process by visiting our classrooms and doing some of the kid watching for us. Figure 5.4 on page 87 shows a format that we have found helpful.

Checklists

Checklists and rubrics (discussed in the next section) share some common characteristics, but checklists do not delve into levels or gradations of achievement or descriptions as rubrics do (Rowlands, 2007). Checklists give the steps in a process or identify traits or features that should be present in a completed product. A checklist for written essays and similar work might look like the one in Figure 5.5. on page 87. Display the checklist on a digital projector, write the list on the whiteboard, or distribute it as a bookmark or sticker.

Some checklists are sequential; that is, the process must be completed in a specific order. Others are requirements checklists that provide a scaffold for organization or cognitive processes. In the example shown in Figure 5.6 on page 87, the checklist serves as a reminder to students of the cognitive moves they can make while writing in a response to literature journal or discussion board. The student responses in this checklist are based on the work of Palincsar and Brown (1981). Checklists may also serve as a foundation or threshold. Student work that does not meet the threshold criteria would not be subject to further assessment.

1. **Participation during whole-class discussion.**
   Participation refers to your comments made and heard by the entire class. Make sure your description is accurate and represents your contribution. What was the context of the discussion?

What did you contribute to whole-class discussion? Report what you shared specifically and your perception of how your thoughts aided the flow of the discussion.	Date:

2. **Participation in pairs, small groups, and project discussions.**
   Participation refers to your comments made and heard by the pair or small group. Make sure your description is accurate and represents your contribution. What was the context of the discussion?

What did you contribute to the pair, small group, and/ or project discussion? Summarize how you participated and your perception of how your thoughts advanced the discussion.	Date:

3. **Self-assessment, reflection, and improvement.**
   Describe your performance as a participant in the class, focusing on your strengths and how you can improve. What did the teacher do to help you engage in discussion, or what might the teacher have done to assist you? Reflect on participation expectations, as well as the quality and quantity of your participation in class.

FIGURE 5.3. Participation log.

From *Assessment Literacy: An Educator's Guide to Understanding Assessment, K–12*, by Thomas DeVere Wolsey, Susan Lenski, and Dana L. Grisham. Copyright © 2020 The Guilford Press. Permission to photocopy this figure is granted to purchasers of this book for personal use or use with students (see copyright page for details). Purchasers can download enlarged versions of this figure (see box at the end of the table of contents).

Date: Focus Students: Purpose:		
What the student does or says:	**What the teacher does or says:**	**Reactions:**
1.		
2.		
3.		

FIGURE 5.4. Kid-watching format.

Response to Literature

How to write a response to literature in your journal:

- Make a prediction about what happens in the next chapter.

- Summarize what you read.

- Summarize what another group member said in discussion.

- Clarify something that previously confused you.

- Ask a question about something that doesn't make sense yet.

- Use a quote from the story to support what you write.

Submission Checklist

Before you submit your assignment, check these features:

1. Is your name in the upper right corner with the date?

2. Did you give your essay a title?

3. Did you make sure that your sources are cited correctly?

4. Did you use the grammar and spelling checker to find any typographic errors?

FIGURE 5.5. Response to literature bookmark.   **FIGURE 5.6.** Submission checklist bookmark.

From *Assessment Literacy: An Educator's Guide to Understanding Assessment, K–12*, by Thomas DeVere Wolsey, Susan Lenski, and Dana L. Grisham. Copyright © 2020 The Guilford Press. Permission to photocopy Figures 5.4, 5.5, and 5.6 is granted to purchasers of this book for personal use or use with students (see copyright page for details). Purchasers can download enlarged versions of this figure (see box at the end of the table of contents).

Rubrics

Rubrics are a popular tool for guiding instruction and aiding teachers and peers to provide feedback to students (e.g., Culham, 2003). Rubrics inform students about the general criteria and expectations for performance, thus increasing transparency about learning goals (e.g., Panadero & Jonsson, 2013). Rubrics are also useful tools for evaluating student work (Goodrich, 1997; Grisham & Wolsey, 2005; Jackson & Larkin, 2002; Montgomery, 2000; Quinlan, 2000). The defining characteristic of a rubric is that it lists criteria against which a performance can be judged, along with descriptions of the levels or gradations of attainment. For this reason, rubrics are often presented as a matrix with the quality gradations across the top and the success criteria in the far-left column. However, there are other ways to present rubrics visually, often as a list of criteria to obtain a specific grade—for example: "A paper earning a grade of 'A' exhibits these characteristics . . ."; "A 'B' paper exhibits these characteristics . . .".

Creating a rubric takes time, but technology can help. Several online sites and apps make rubric creation seamless and relatively easy:

- *TeAchnology* offers rubrics (but you'll need to register) available at *www.teach-nology.com/web_tools/rubrics*.
- *RubiStar*, a project of ALTEC, has a useful rubric generator available at *http://rubistar.4teachers.org*.
- The Google add-in by *dostuffgood.org* allows you to create and send customizable rubrics and scores to students by email for any assignment and is available at *https://gsuite.google.com/marketplace/app/online_rubric/546147263043*.

Figure 5.7 shows an example of a rubric for evaluating a narrative summary (McCormack & Pasquarelli, 2010). The quality indicators in rubrics are sometimes presented as numbers, with 1 being a poor performance and 4 being an exemplary performance, for example. Other efforts to make quality indicators more student friendly and motivating use indicators such as "approaching grade level," "on grade level," and so forth, or "meets standard," "nearly meets standard," "exceeds standard," as in Figure 5.7. Other indicators include "emerging, developing, proficient, and exemplary." Often, the learning target is represented in the second column (number 3, on grade level, meets standard, proficient), with particularly excellent performances in the first column presented as a challenge for which students might aspire to or reach.

Rubrics are of two general types. *Analytic rubrics* assign a value to each cell in the matrix, and a score is then derived by summing up the points from each cell. Care must be taken in creating analytic rubrics not to place too much weight on criteria that would overshadow others. *Holistic rubrics* do not distribute points across the criteria and quality indicators. Instead, holistic rubrics require the teacher to

Score each bulleted item separately.

	4 Exceeds standard	3 Meets standard	2 Nearly meets standard	1–0 Below standard
Content	• Summary contains accurate information that matches the original text. • Summary contains concise inclusion of all story elements. • Summary contains concise inclusion of all important plot details. • Summary contains no redundant or trivial ideas.	• Summary contains some inaccurate information that does not match the original text. • Summary contains all story elements. • Summary contains all important plot details. • Summary contains one idea that is redundant or trivial.	• Summary contains significant inaccurate information that does not match the original text. • Summary contains most story elements. • Summary contains most important plot details. • Summary contains a few ideas that are redundant or trivial.	• Summary contains so much inaccurate information that a new graphic organizer must be completed and the summary must be rewritten. • Summary is missing too many story elements and must be rewritten. • Summary is missing too many important plot details and must be rewritten. • Summary needs a full revision to delete redundant or trivial details.
Organization	• Very well organized; text structure appropriate for topic. • Clear transitions are used to make the summary cohesive.	• Organized; text structure appropriate for topic. • Some transitions are used to make the summary cohesive.	• Weak organization or text structure does not match topic. • The summary needs revision to include transitions to help with cohesiveness.	• Poorly organized or no text structure. • The summary needs complete revision for cohesiveness.
Sentence structure and conventions	• Well-developed sentences with good variety of sentence beginnings. • Few or no errors in spelling, grammar, or punctuation.	• Most sentences are well developed with some variety in sentence beginnings. • Some grammatical errors, but they do not interfere with meaning.	• Some run-on or incomplete sentences with little variety in sentence beginnings. • Several grammar errors that make writing unclear.	• Many run-ons or incomplete sentences with no variety in sentence beginnings. • Grammatical errors interfere with readers' understanding.
Writing process	• All stages of the process are included. • Graphic organizers are complete and detailed. • Significant growth from draft to draft.	• Most stages of the process are included. • Graphic organizers are complete but not detailed. • Shows adequate growth from draft to draft.	• Some stages of the process are included. • Incomplete graphic organizers that led to lack of information in the summary. • Shows little or no growth from draft to draft.	• No stages of the process are included. • No graphic organizers included. • There is only one draft.

FIGURE 5.7. Example of a rubric for narrative summaries. From McCormack and Pasquarelli (2010). Copyright © 2010 The Guilford Press. Reprinted with permission.

From McCormack and Pasquarelli (2010). Copyright © 2010 The Guilford Press. Reprinted by permission in *Assessment Literacy: An Educator's Guide to Understanding Assessment, K–12*, by Thomas DeVere Wolsey, Susan Lenski, and Dana L. Grisham (The Guilford Press, 2020). Permission to photocopy this figure is granted to purchasers of this book for personal use or use with students (see copyright page for details). Purchasers can download enlarged versions of this figure (see box at the end of the table of contents).

assign an overall grade based on the rubric criteria. In both types of rubrics, the teacher generally marks the cell representing the level of quality and criteria, often adding in additional comments for clarification.

Rubrics are often time-consuming to create because the teacher must identify what the success criteria are, and then delineate all the levels of performance for each one of them. Effective teachers typically refine their rubrics after each use. Often students do something that is not specifically contained in the rubric and, in these cases, teachers write in additional comments as feedback. Many teachers find that students (Grisham & Wolsey, 2005) are quite capable of identifying the characteristics of a good performance, and they learn how to enhance that performance by creating the rubrics themselves with teacher guidance.

Rubrics are useful prior to student performance of a task, such as an oral presentation or writing assignment, because students can see what the expectations are, and as students work they are useful as a guide to the creation of the performance or product. Finally, they are useful as a tool for providing feedback from peers and from the teacher during a stop-and-check step of the process or once the product or performance is completed.

Of course, rubrics can also be combined with other instruments or performances. Students may use a rubric for peer review of their work or to guide their performance on a presentation. What is a rubric, after all? A box—or, rather, a series of boxes inside a box. Crazy as it sounds, sometimes teachers actually want their students to think *inside* the box; that is, to use the exemplars, anchors, and models to identify what the rubric is asking the students to do. At other times, we may want students to think *beyond* the box, or to recognize gradations that a rubric with a lot of text may not capture. Two modifications of rubrics that allow more flexibility—the *sliding scale rubric* and the *single-point rubric*—might be of interest to you.

The sliding scale rubric offers flexibility because the target is described and then the criterion is scored based on how close the performance or task is to the target. We show an example of a rubric using a sliding set of arrows in Figure 5.9 (see p. 92). This rubric might also be used to show student growth by indicating the level of proficiency before the student begins a similar task. For example, Michael may have received 7s and 8s on most of the criteria the last time he was asked to write; the next time, he marks those numbers on the scale and then works to improve his performance.

On this sliding scale rubric, the criteria on the left are representative of an exemplary performance, which is the goal that students ought to achieve. The sliding rubric also has a little more room for written feedback.

Another variation of the traditional matrix is called the single-point rubric (Fluckiger, 2010) (see an example in Figure 5.10 on p. 93). The single-point rubric places the target criteria (e.g., on grade level) in the middle column. Columns to the left and right leave room for more substantive written feedback from the teacher.

The flexibility of the single-point rubric recognizes that feedback is based on whether a product, such as an argumentative or opinion essay, "meets" or "skillfully meets" the requirements. The teacher is free to address the nuances of the student's work in a more detailed manner.

Constructing the Rubrics

For comparison, let's construct a rubric of each type. Figure 5.8 shows an example of a traditional matrix-type rubric. We focus on three success criteria because our purpose is to demonstrate how the different rubrics are constructed. We can turn this traditional rubric into a sliding scale rubric by focusing on the first level of characteristics or descriptors, as in Figure 5.9. Or we can convert the traditional rubric into a single-point rubric by focusing on the second-level column, as in Figure 5.10 on page 93. Notice that the position of the descriptors is visually important in the sliding scale and single-point rubrics depending on which descriptors you want your students to focus on. If you want to set a challenging target, the most challenging set of descriptors will fit the format of the sliding scale rubric. If

	Exemplary	Proficient	Developing	Emerging
Comprehension and use of text-based evidence	• Takes a position. • Supports position with citations and examples from the text. • Includes other points of view.	• Position implied. • Supports position with some citations and examples that may not be fully described.	• Partially takes a position or summarizes the text. • Provides minimal support using citations and examples.	• Summarizes the text without support from the text.
Idea development	• Fully developed connections to other literature. • Vocabulary choices are above grade level. • Logical organization that flows.	• May describe connections to other literature. • Uses vocabulary choices that are expected at grade level. • Logical organization.	• Few or no connections to other literature. • Vocabulary choices are routine. • Organization is lacking or confusing.	• No connections to other literature. • Vocabulary choices are thin. • Organization is confusing or not evident.
Conventions	• Nearly flawless spelling and punctuation. • Varied sentence structures.	• Some spelling and punctuation errors that don't interfere with reading. • Uses some variation of sentence structures.	• Many spelling or punctuation errors interfere with reading. • Sentence structures are not varied.	• Many spelling or punctuation errors make the paper very difficult to read. • Sentence structures are surface-level.

FIGURE 5.8. Example of a traditional rubric in a matrix.

you want to focus on meeting a particular standard or set of standards, the single-point rubric is a good choice.

 Trickster trap: Sometimes rubrics aren't the magic bullet they are made out to be. Maja Wilson (2006, 2007/2008) believes rubrics can be limiting because they encompass such a small number of criteria. For example, the 6 + 1 Trait rubric (Northwest Regional Educational Laboratory, 2001) identifies these traits: ideas, organization, voice, word choice, sentence fluency, and conventions. The "plus one" trait in 6 + 1 is presentation. Wilson notes that the generic nature of the criteria and the limited focus on these six areas are problems inherent in this rubric.

Another study of written products in first-year college English (Broad, 2003) found more than 89 categories of values held by teaching assistants, adjunct

	Exemplary	Proficient	Developing	Emerging
Comprehension and use of text-based evidence: • Takes a position. • Supports position with citations and examples from the text. • Includes other points of view.	10 9 8	7 6 5	4 3	2 1 *Notes and comments here.*
Idea development: • Fully developed connections to other literature. • Vocabulary choices are above grade level. • Logical organization that flows.	10 9 8	7 6 5	4 3	2 1
Conventions: • Nearly flawless spelling and punctuation. • Varied sentence structures.	10 9 8	7 6 5	4 3	2 1
Notes: Total points:				

FIGURE 5.9. Example of a sliding scale rubric for response to literature.

Suggestions and Challenges *What are your next steps?*	Criteria *Standards for Response to Literature*	Advanced *What is the evidence that this response to literature has exceeded the standard?*
	Criterion 1: Comprehension and use of text-based evidence • Position implied. • Supports position with some citations and examples that may not be fully described.	
	Criterion 2: Idea development • May describe connections to other literature. • Uses vocabulary choices that are expected at grade level. • Logical organization.	
	Criterion 3: Conventions • Some spelling and punctuation errors that don't interfere with reading. • Uses some variation of sentence structures.	

FIGURE 5.10. Example of a single-point rubric for response to literature.

professors, and full-time faculty about students' writing. These values were then categorized as follows:

- 46 textual criteria, including two subcategories
- 31 textual qualities, such as significance and audience awareness
- 15 textual features, such as paragraphing, spelling, and content
- 22 contextual values, including the purpose of the writing task and course goals
- 21 scoring task values, such as scoring samples

Because writing is such a complex undertaking, Broad (2003) points out that the 89 criteria he identified shouldn't be used to create a checklist or rubric. Besides, your school faculty might hold values that are different from those of the professors and teaching assistants in his study. What does all this mean? One conclusion is that not every aspect of writing that a student might need to develop can be captured on a rubric. Often, what students need is the expert guidance of a teacher who knows the craft of writing (or any other type of performance, such as a lab assignment or a presentation). Recall our discussion of the importance of relationships in Chapter 3.

Learning Progressions

Based on the notion of *design thinking* (see *https://tll.gse.harvard.edu/design-thinking*), another approach called *learning progressions* considers standards and developmental progress. Design thinking focuses on inquiry and processes, not just the product or task. Learning progressions are often stated in terms of ability, of what students can do, rather than what they cannot do. Educational work in Australia continues to create learning progressions for reading and mathematics.[1] Meanwhile, we can implement the idea in our classrooms. Because rubrics are often (but not always) created by an outside assessor (the teacher, the school board, etc.), they contain criteria that may not seem approachable for students trying to understand and implement whatever the learning is intended to be. Take a look at this "I can" learning progression from the CCSS.

> *Distinguish among facts, reasoned judgment based on research findings, and speculation in a text.*
>
>> Level 4: I can assess the extent to which the reasoning and evidence in the article we read to support the author's recommendation for solving a scientific or technical problem.
>> Level 3: I can identify and list relevant facts in the article we read, and I can explain how the author used these facts to make a judgement based on research and describe how and where the author speculates beyond the facts given.
>> Level 2: I can identify facts the author used and explain how the author arrived at a judgement based on research.
>> Level 1: I can identify facts the author used and explain the main idea the author was trying to convey.
>> (NGA & CCSSO, 2010 [CCSS.ELA-Literacy.RST.6-8.8])

As you can see, the levels are based on a specific standard, and in our example the "I can" levels are linked to a specific learning task related to reading an article from a scientific magazine or journal. The CCSS are themselves a learning progression from grade band to grade band, so to construct this example, we used grades 9–10 standards in the Integration of Knowledge and Ideas strand to construct the top level in the learning progression.

In this example, there are no fifth-grade standards that align because the writing standards for the sciences and technical subjects begin at grade six. However, for many of the standards, you may want to look at the skills and dispositions above and below your target grade level to create knowledge progressions to guide your students. Knowing your students and the content and processes you teach are vital elements in constructing classroom-specific learning progressions that are granular enough to be applied by students and challenging enough that they can learn and understand how they are making progress. In what ways can you see how learning

---

[1] Learn more about this work at *www.acer.org/au/gem/learning-progression-explorer*.

progressions might present a viable and inquiry-driven approach to assessment compared to rubrics—or the other way around? In what ways might feedback be used with learning progressions to promote successively better iterations of the process, product, or performance?

Portfolios

One of the most effective tools for showing growth over time and for displaying the best learning a student has done may be the *portfolio*. Artists are very familiar with portfolios, and we can learn something about how to create successful portfolios by looking at how artists prepare them. Many of our readers will be familiar with The College Board's Advanced Placement (AP) examinations that allow high school students to demonstrate proficiency in different subject areas, usually with a written examination. The AP art exam is different, however. In AP studio art and its iterations, students select artwork that they created that demonstrates in-depth or sustained investigation of an art form. The portfolios cannot be machine scored, so they are instead evaluated by three to seven artist-educators with experience in the type of art submitted by the student.[2]

Portfolios make the assessment stories our students tell interesting, and even fascinating, because with a portfolio the hero of the story is in control of her or his destiny. Portfolios allow students time to prepare and the opportunity to select what work represents them and their educational outcomes best. Deborah Meier, founder of Mission Hill K–8 School in Massachusetts and of the Central Park East schools in New York City, is a fierce advocate for building education for democracy around the notion of community. She writes:

> The work produced by Central Park East students, for example, is collected regularly in portfolios; it is examined (and in the case of high school students, judged) by tough internal and external reviewers, in a process that closely resembles a doctoral dissertation oral exam. The standards by which a student is judged are easily accessible to families, clear to kids, and capable of being judged by other parties. (Meier, 2000, "Accountability," para. 7)

Portfolios are a collection of work that demonstrate mastery of objectives and standards, but they also reflect the choices (at least the best ones do) of the students. Like many of the assessment tools described here, portfolios can be combined with checklists, rubrics, observation protocols, and so on. They may also be used formatively and summatively. In language arts classes, students may include responses to literature, examples of opinion or argumentative writing, creative writing, rubrics from oral presentations, or even videos of those presentations. The

---

[2] Learn more at *https://apstudent.collegeboard.org/apcourse/ap-studio-art-2-d-design/course-details*.

digital possibilities are endless, and include being able to share students' work with parents, other classes, and even the world.

Portfolios are useful tools for showing a process (such as successive drafts of an essay), progress (such as including a reading log showing how more complex texts are read from the beginning of the year), or for demonstrating mastery of a particular skill, genre, and so on. In our experience, portfolios that students make public, for more than just the teacher and classmates, also inspire students to put forth their best work.

I (Dana) was a elementary school teacher in the 1980s. During that time I also attended the National Writing Project, which had a profound influence on my teaching, and in fact on my life, in a very positive way. This experience led me to graduate education and to a terminal degree in curriculum and instruction. I then left the public school classroom for teacher preparation at the university.

The experience of the summer writing program introduced me to new colleagues, a new and more connected longitudinal view of K–12 education, and an enduring interest in writing instruction. During the 6-week-long writing program, I learned to question my own practice and to refine my questions about it. Dr. Dan Donlan served as my mentor and ultimately as my doctoral advisor. It was a summer of bliss for me!

One of the ideas I encountered was the idea of portfolio assessment, or "seeing writing assessment as progress" (Huot & Neal, 2006). In this view of writing instruction, the authors viewed the process of writing as one of continuing growth. In my third-grade classroom, I decided to improve my writing instruction by viewing it with my students as a sort of journey over the school year. Beginning in early September (when school always used to start), I would ask my students to write about their summer—an overused topic, I know. We used the writing process approach.

First, for the prewriting and generation of ideas, I shared what I did with my own children over the summer. Then, in cooperative learning groups, the children shared their summer experiences with each other. We began drafting our stories by drawing pictures or creating text or both. Then the students again shared with their group. As the teacher, I met with each group to give a little teacher feedback, focusing on each student's strengths and needs. After students did their revisions, they once again shared. A second round of revision took place, then editing for errors. (Note: In editing we focused on one or two issues the students shared.) Finally, students completed their final draft. Several of the students volunteered to share their writing with the whole class.

In terms of assessment, the students provided a score for each other based on what they liked about the story. Then I provided a summative assessment for each child, stating specific positives, such as their observation of using capitals to start a sentence, which was a major issue for third grade, then making suggestions for improvement. Each student then took responsibility for putting his or her completed writing in a portfolio (a cardboard folder in those days) that I collected and kept in a filing cabinet for future writing.

Our academic year continued with the ongoing writing workshop. As students completed writing assignments—some of their own choice and some structured by me as the teacher—they were included in the portfolio. Conferences with students (and sometimes the parent) saw us referring back to the writing and pointing out growth in two to three areas, and I would ask the student where she or he thought improvement might be needed. Sometimes, I would be the one making a suggestion for improvement. Together, we would write a note that went into the portfolio.

The strength of this process came from the fact that students could evaluate their own progress. The student became an agent, not a subject. In this way, the portfolio experience gave them a sense of writing as ongoing and developing. For me as the teacher, it served as a reminder that third graders were capable of self-evaluation. In conferences, I was able to communicate with parents about their children's growth using data collected over time. Even though portfolio assessment requires consistency and is time-consuming, overall, in looking at the process, I believe the effort was worth it.

Are you considering a digital portfolio for your students? There are so many options—just type in "digital portfolio" into any search engine, and you will have a plethora of choices. To help narrow the options, we developed a series of questions that may guide your digital portfolio choices and options.

- Will the infrastructure (bandwidth, Internet filters, Wi-Fi, etc.) support the digital portfolio initiative you have planned?
- Do students have access to computers, tablets, and other technology?
- What costs are involved in purchasing hardware, apps, scanners, and other tools?
- What training do you and your students need to make the best use of the technology?
- How do digital portfolios fit with your curriculum?
- Does the technology support learning, or are students just using the technology because it is more engaging?
- How will you and your students make the portfolios public? Are there any school policies about using students' names online? (Be sure to read the section in Chapter 8 about federal laws regarding privacy as well.)
- How will you, students, parents, and the public give affirmations or other feedback?

Magician tip: Jefferson County Public Schools in Kentucky use portfolios, but they call them virtual backpacks (Schlemmer, 2019). Students in fifth and eighth grades and high school seniors prepare a backpack that they present to a panel of administrators and parents. Using digital tools, they show artifacts in their virtual backpacks. At Kammerer Middle School, eighth graders present selected artifacts that show how they meet the school goals of being prepared and resilient learners, being globally and culturally responsive citizens, being innovative, being effective communicators, and being productive collaborators. The results help teachers, students, and parents transcend the traditional teach–test paradigm.

Presentations

A few years ago, we (Dana and Thomas) and our colleagues Diane Lapp and Javier Vaca from Health Sciences High and Middle College in San Diego (2014) explored digital *eposters*. The idea of the eposter is to make use of various online tools that help students summarize their research concisely and in a visually appealing way. The eposter is displayed online, and students may then navigate around the eposters and provide feedback, ask questions, and engage with the poster creators much as they would in a face-to-face setting. Students might also create infographics. Students found that to be concise in creating an eposter, they had to read and reread the sources in order to fully understand the content before they could represent it online. We found that the 11th-grade students were employing their skills with close reading to be as accurate as possible, while providing enough information so that rich discussion could occur among their peers.

Figure 5.11 shows a fragment of a student-created poster synthesizing research on the annexation of Hawaii to the United States. Students used Glogster for this

FIGURE 5.11. Student poster on the annexation of Hawaii, created using Glogster. From Grisham, Lapp, Wolsey, and Vaca (2014). Copyright © 2014 Kean University. Reprinted by permission.

project (see *https://edu.glogster.com*), but many options are available. You may want to try one of the tools in Figure 5.12.

As with other formative assessment techniques, it is often useful to combine tools. For example, if students work on teams to create an eposter, it may be a good idea to also use the Goal 18 tool (Figure 5.13) to foster increasingly cooperative behavior, along with a checklist or learning progressions for the content and presentation of the poster. Groups discuss and agree on a rating—3, 2, or 1—for the task and the group processes. The total possible for each column is 9, and the total possible for both is 18.

Many of these ideas are also transferable to other face-to-face presentations in class with a slide deck, a role-play performance, or a demonstration. Several features of presentations that might be included in a rubric are:

* Pitch
* Enthusiasm
* Speaks clearly
* Uses complete sentences
* Evaluates peers
* Content

* Pauses
* Attire
* Props
* Stays on topic
* Time limit
* Volume

* Comprehension
* Preparedness
* Vocabulary
* Posture and eye contact
* Listens to other presentations
* Collaborates with peers

Tool	URL	Description/Features
Voicethread	*http://voicethread.com*	A collaborative Web-based application and social networking tool where individuals may upload many kinds of media to present and/or respond to in five ways using voice (with a mic or telephone), text, audio file, or video (via a webcam).
Prezi	*http://prezi.com*	Prezi is a presentation tool that helps you organize and present ideas with art, media, and interconnectivity. Prezi provides nonlinear and zooming movement in presentations and can be used for collaboration in meetings.
PowerPoint	*http://office.microsoft.com/en-us/powerpoint*	PowerPoint is seemingly ubiquitous; however, it is almost universally viewable, and it has the capability of integrating sound, images, and text. Moreover, PowerPoint slides can be uploaded to file-sharing sites (e.g., *www.authorstream.com* and *Slideshare.net*). Newer versions also permit PowerPoints to be converted into narrated video that can be uploaded to sites such as YouTube.
Glogster	*www.glogster.com*	Glogster is a social and visualizing network presentation tool that allows you to express your ideas by connecting and "mashing up" your favorite media, photo, and video sites to express your ideas. You can rotate, resize, and add effects and animations with Glogster tools. Glogster is the site name, and Glog is the poster tool created there.

FIGURE 5.12. Presentation tools. From Grisham, Lapp, Wolsey, and Vaca (2014). Copyright © 2014 Kean University. Adapted by permission.

The task Yes = 3; almost = 2; no = 1			The group Yes = 3; almost = 2; no = 1
• Task is done.			• Everyone helped.
• On time.			• Pleased with the work.
• Done right.			• Ready for the next task.
Task total			Group total
Job + Group =			

FIGURE 5.13. Goal 18 group-evaluation tool.

From *Assessment Literacy: An Educator's Guide to Understanding Assessment, K–12,* by Thomas DeVere Wolsey, Susan Lenski, and Dana L. Grisham. Copyright © 2020 The Guilford Press. Permission to photocopy this figure is granted to purchasers of this book for personal use or use with students (see copyright page for details). Purchasers can download enlarged versions of this figure (see box at the end of the table of contents).

STORIES FROM RESEARCH (AND THE MOVIES)

Danny Brassell, PhD, a Faculty Advisor at CalStateTEACH, is a longtime colleague and friend of the authors. Danny has the unique ability to motivate people to action. Readers of this book will be interested in how we can motivate our students to read both widely and deeply. We asked Danny to tell us a little about how using students' reading interests can make reading fun.

Making Reading Assessment Fun and Meaningful

DANNY BRASSELL

There's a scene in the movie *Big* with Tom Hanks (Ross, Spielberg, & Marshall, 1988) in which the Tom Hanks character, Josh (a young boy trapped in the body of an adult), attends a meeting at the toy company where he works. He listens to an executive present an idea for a toy that transforms from a building into a robot, then raises his hand and innocently asks, "What's fun about that?" The executive is perturbed that anyone would have the audacity to question him during his presentation, so he hands Josh a printout of marketing research. The bewildered Josh raises his hand again, and he repeats, "But what's fun about that?"

Welcome to public education! So often we adults, though mostly well intentioned, miss the point. We create activities and assessments that *we* think are engaging for students, without considering their needs and interests. And an unintended but often seen circumstance is disengaged students.

Reading instruction is no different. Most public schools do a decent job of teaching kids how to read. However, what good is teaching kids *how* to read if they never *want* to read? Engagement is key, and the right assessments will help teachers and parents alike in individualizing student reading instruction based on student interests rather than on district, state, and federal mandates.

In this commentary, I consider three basic questions. First, why should we assess students' interest in reading? I examine the reasons we should find out about students' reading *attitudes,* as opposed to just their *aptitudes,* in determining the reading *altitudes* students can reach. Second, what are beneficial ways to assess students' interest in reading? I briefly discuss some of the most useful assessment tools we have observed in classrooms. Finally, how do we use these reading interest assessments? Let's look at ways to use assessments as useful feedback that guides our instruction and supports interest in reading.

By assessing students' reading interests in engaging and meaningful ways, our goals are (1) to provide educators and parents useful feedback in how to design reading programs that are most beneficial to each student and (2) to motivate students to reflect on their reading habits and increase their awareness of how to become more engaged readers.

Why Should We Assess Students' Interest in Reading?

When most people think about reading assessment, they think about measuring students' proficiency in reading. Indeed, for educators and parents alike, it is important to understand what students know, what they are learning at a given moment, and what they have learned. So, when assessing reading, we need to assess to find out students' reading proficiency level before we teach, frequently check students' progress while we teach, and then make sure students have mastered what we have taught (Afflerbach, 2007). Understanding a student's reading aptitude is absolutely critical.

However, one of the best indicators of reading aptitude lies in reading frequency, and frequency is a function of attitude. Reading researchers have found that the volume of leisure reading is a crucial factor in a student's success. A report by the National Institute of Child Health and Human Development (2000) affirmed that literally hundreds of correlational studies find that the best readers read the most, that poor readers read the least, and that the more children read, the better their fluency, vocabulary, and comprehension.

Put simply, interest in reading can tell us a lot about a student's proficiency in reading. Too often, this phenomenon is ignored.

There's an old saying in real estate that the three essential components to purchasing a property are location, location, location. Similarly, reading research suggests that there are three keys to improving reading: reading, reading, reading. In fact, researchers have found that high reading volume isn't a *result* of high reading ability but rather a *source* of high reading ability (Cunningham & Stanovich, 2003). So how do we find out how much students read, and how do we encourage them to read?

Research on reading motivation demonstrates the need to engage students as they develop into independent, committed readers (Afflerbach, Pearson, & Paris, 2008; Guthrie & Klauda, 2016). Students read more when they are interested, and the more they read, the better they get at it (Cunningham & Stanovich, 1998; Gambrell, 2011). And as students get better at reading, the more they want to do it (Wigfield & Guthrie, 1997). So, when educators and parents understand students' degree of interest in reading, the more data they have in determining personalized reading plans that build on students' unique interests.

What Are Beneficial Ways to Assess Students' Interest in Reading?

Determining the interests of students is essential in assisting them to become better readers, as teachers and parents can foster resources and activities that cater to students' desire to deepen their knowledge about specific content.

> The interests of the student are paramount in assessment. . . . First and foremost, assessment must encourage students to become engaged in literacy learning, to reflect on their own reading and writing in productive ways, and to set respective literacy goals. In this way, students become involved in, and responsible for, their own learning and are better able to assist the teacher in focusing instruction. . . . Specific information on students' (attitudes) helps teachers, parents, and students set goals and plan instruction more thoughtfully. . . . The context in which (these assessments) are used can be equally important. Indeed, the most productive and powerful assessments for students are likely to be the formative assessments that occur in the daily activities of the classroom. (Joint Task Force on Assessment of the International Reading Association and the National Council of Teachers of English, 2016, pp. 18–19)

Many students struggle with reading because classroom reading resources are too difficult or are of little interest. Other students—reluctant readers—have the necessary reading skills but choose not to read because they do not find it to be an enjoyable activity. We know that children who read independently and frequently become better readers (Taylor, Frye, & Maruyama, 1990). And one of the best ways to promote frequent reading is to build on specific student reading interests so they can deepen their background knowledge (Adams, 2011).

Reading Frequency Surveys

Reading volume is critical to reading proficiency (Cunningham & Stanovich, 1998), and it has been demonstrated consistently that volume increases when student interest is higher (Cox & Guthrie, 2001). So, examining the frequency with which students read can provide teachers with greater insights into how interested students are in reading.

Interest Inventories

Teachers must determine students' reading interests. Interest inventories provide teachers with insights into what appropriate reading materials to provide students. Researchers have observed that the assessments themselves are far less important than the reading materials students are presented with (Renninger & Bachrach, 2015).

Individual Reading Conferences

These interviews are brief one-on-one sessions in which teachers and students discuss what students are reading. By better understanding the topics students want to learn more about, teachers are better equipped to direct students to appropriate reading materials (Springer, Harris, & Dole, 2017).

HOW DO WE USE THESE READING INTEREST ASSESSMENTS?

Many schools could improve their performance by establishing better ways to utilize the information gathered through reading-interest assessments and formulating reading programs that can address any deficiencies. Put simply, schools can best help struggling and reluctant readers when they use this information to improve their teaching, rather than to label children as inadequate in certain areas.

The goal of teaching reading is to develop efficient and self-motivated readers. Therefore, educators should promote positive reading attitudes through enjoyable reading experiences. Realizing that when children spend time reading their ability to read improves, teachers need to find ways to encourage children to read more in school and at home. Multiple studies show that supporting students' reading interests has a positive impact on their reading development (Schunk & Mullen, 2009). Four simple, but proven, ways to support student reading interests are allowing time for silent reading, offering a choice of reading materials, providing appropriate adult modeling of reading, and sharing of literature read with and by children (Moser & Morrison, 1998).

Allowing Time for Silent Reading

Sustained silent reading (SSR) is allotted time for students to read self-selected books. By allowing students to select their own books, teachers allow them to find materials that interest them, which has been shown to improve their reading motivation and experience (Gardiner, 2001; Hiebert & Reutzel, 2010). When students are given time in school to read materials of their choosing, they tend to be more engaged and enjoy reading more.

Offering a Choice of Reading Materials

Iyengar and Lepper (2000) found that students who had been given a greater selection of reading materials expressed higher levels of satisfaction with their choices compared to those who had no choice. Further studies suggest that allowing students broader choices in their overall learning enhances their determination, ownership, motivation, and involvement (Vitto, 2003).

Providing Appropriate Adult Modeling of Reading

Interactive read-alouds are critical because they allow teachers additional opportunities to engage students in reading (Wiseman, 2011), often outside what students have identified as their interest. One of the key benefits of reading aloud to students is providing them with a model of how to read the text, which boosts the confidence of students when they attempt to read the texts independently. By providing students with support through modeling and questioning, teachers can gradually withdraw their support, as students transition from guided practice to independent practice (Pentimonti & Justice, 2010).

Sharing Literature Read with and by Children

The benefits of reading aloud to students extend far beyond students having a reading role model. Read-alouds are also ideal for stimulating interactive discussions that permit teachers to assist students in a variety of ways, from connecting text with students' own lives to refuting any misconceptions students have about what they read (Strachan, 2015).

SO, WHAT'S FUN ABOUT THAT?

The way students improve their reading is by reading more, and the way to get students to read more is to reinforce it around student interests. Again, what good is it teaching students *how* to read if they never *want* to read?

Assessing students' interest in reading is critical in developing an optimal program to facilitate their growth in reading. Reading engagement models that examine what students are interested in and how frequently they choose to read outside of school can help teachers develop programs that make reading fun, meaningful, and memorable for students so that they choose to do it on their own.

Very few students need to be told to watch television or to play video games. So why should reading be any different? Teachers and parents need to promote reading as a reward in itself. Let's create an environment where students are never instructed to read but rather choose to do it freely on their own.

PREASSESSMENT TOOLS

Assessment *before* learning is a topic that doesn't receive much attention, but it should. How, you might wonder, is it possible to assess learning before the learning events have occurred? In Chapter 3 we talked about assessment for learning and the role of formative assessment that permits the teacher to enter a dialogue with learners. Students do not arrive in our classrooms as empty containers waiting for us to fill them up with useful knowledge and skills, right? What we need to tap is what they already know in order to reinforce the strengths they have when they walk through the door.

Teachers frequently use knowledge or vocabulary rating charts to determine just how much students know about a concept as represented by vocabulary terms (see Dale & O'Rourke, 1981) using a self-assessment strategy. Students mark their responses for each term prior to reading (or listening or viewing), then return to the knowledge rating chart after reading to indicate how well they now grasp the ideas represented by the vocabulary term. See Figure 5.14 for an example.

Preassessing what students already know prior to instruction has many benefits. Teachers can build on what students know instead of guessing based on what classes the students took the previous year. You may recall our discussion, "My students should 'know' this," in Chapter 4 (pp. 68–69). Students get a broad overview of what the lesson, unit, or course will be covering, and they can look for concepts they don't know well, instead of focusing on those they already know. Another useful tool is the anticipation guide (Dufflemeyer, 1994). Websites in both English and Spanish explain how to use anticipation guides and provide reproducible resources.[3]

Word	I can define it or use it.	I can tell you something about it.	Think I've heard of it.	I have no idea.
Egyptologist				
Pharaoh				
Imhotep				
Mummy				
Pyramid				
Memphis				
Vizier				

FIGURE 5.14. Example of a knowledge rating chart for ancient Egypt.

[3] For more on anticipation guides in English: *www.readwritethink.org/classroom-resources/printouts/anticipation-guide-30578.html*; and in Spanish: *https://literacybeat.com/2018/03/23/anticipation-guides-guias-de-anticipacion.*

When I (Thomas) was a seventh grader in Utah a long time ago, students were required to take a course in the history of the state. I was fortunate to have Mr. Gourdin as a teacher, who took his teaching seriously but knew how to make learning fun. Mr. Gourdin knew that most of his class had lived in the state all or nearly all of their lives, so we knew stuff about it. Before each unit, Mr. Gourdin gave us a pretest, which gave him information about what we already knew. It also piqued our interest about what we might learn. It may seem odd that I actually remember the pretest quizzes, but I do!

Knowledge surveys work in much the same manner. Usually, they are given at the beginning of a course, learning module, or unit. The distinguishing feature of a knowledge survey is to determine if students believe that they are capable of answering the question, not whether the students actually can do so. The National Association of Geoscience Teachers has compiled a number of resources, including a bank of survey questions, for a variety of courses in the field of geoscience.[4] Their survey questions may serve as a model to guide you in creating knowledge surveys for your own subject areas and grade levels.

Each knowledge survey question is keyed to Bloom's revised taxonomy (Anderson & Krathwohl, 2001). At the end of the semester (and sometimes at the midpoint), students take the same survey again. They are awarded one survey point for each "not confident" response, two points for each "possibly confident" response, and three points for each "confident" response. Of course, these points are given for the purpose of gathering information about what students know, not for assigning grades. Because the students are only indicating how confident they feel about their knowledge, many more questions can be asked that can give the instructor a broad overview of what students know or believe they know at the outset.

In preparing a knowledge survey, teachers also have an opportunity for self-assessment of their teaching. By keying the questions to Bloom's revised taxonomy, instructors can determine how often and to what extent they are targeting the upper range of cognitive skills and how often they are addressing only the lower range. Students may use the presurvey as a study guide during the course and as an indicator of how well they believe they are prepared just before a summative assessment, such as an examination, to identify any gaps in their understandings (Wirth & Perkins, 2005).

Take a look at the examples below of the types of statements one might make related to a CCSS literacy standard, this time relative to Bloom's revised taxonomy (adapted from Wirth & Perkins, 2005). In a fourth-grade class studying myths and fables, students are working toward achieving CCSS. ELA-Literacy.RL.4.9: *Compare and contrast the treatment of similar themes and topics (e.g., opposition of good and evil) and patterns of events (e.g., the quest) in stories, myths, and traditional literature*

---

[4]Find them at *https://serc.carleton.edu/NAGTWorkshops/assess/knowledgesurvey/resources.html.*

from different cultures. Some of the knowledge survey questions might be based on the following statements:

- I can define what a fable's characteristics are (Bloom's level: Remembering).
- I can compare fables from two different cultures (Bloom's level: Understanding).
- I can apply fables to my own life (Bloom's level: Applying).
- I can classify fables based on their themes (Bloom's level: Analyzing).
- I can explain why fables were important in past civilizations (Bloom's level: Evaluating).
- I can create a fable for modern times (Bloom's level: Creating).

Notice that these statements are written from the "I can" perspective. In this way, they nudge students to think about what they can do instead of what their deficits may be.

STUDENT-CREATED ARTIFACTS

Nearly anything that students produce or do can be assessed. For convenience, we call the entire idea of work products, processes, and performances by one name: *artifacts.* As we have pointed out throughout this book, assessment need not be a separate event from instruction. When it comes to formative assessments, the principle we recommend is that what students do and what they produce during instruction is an assessment event at the same time. Sometimes, these artifacts, when used for assessment *and* instruction, are called "embedded assessments."

Drawings and visualizations, for example, can help students understand a concept, while also permitting the teacher to observe the depth of understanding. In the journal page shown in Figure 5.15, a student skillfully reconstructs how Santiago in *The Old Man and the Sea* (Hemingway, 1952) has set his fishing lines. By drawing a picture, the student has constructed a visual understanding of what he is reading in the book, and the teacher has visual evidence that the student does indeed understand what he is reading.

Similarly, graphic organizers are tools students use to categorize and organize information in order to understand concepts more effectively, and they are also useful assessment tools for the teacher. Case studies, projects (such as creating a public service announcement), service learning, role-plays, and demonstrations are all examples of instructional activities for students that also provide assessment information.

FIGURE 5.15. A sample student journal page on *The Old Man and the Sea*.

PEER REVIEW AND GROUPWORK

Peer review or peer assistance has a well-documented effect on writing instruction (see Graham & Perrin, 2007), especially during revision phases (see Emig, 1971). When students are taught to use the tools we have discussed previously, they increase their own knowledge of just what a good performance might look like. For example, using a learning progression or rubric, students can be critical friends who help each other improve the quality of their respective work and processes while becoming adept at understanding them as well. Planning, drafting, devising, revising, editing, and considering the strengths of the group are all valuable activities that can be done as a peer-reviewed or peer-supported activity. We agree with Cohen (1994) that group norms and roles can and should be taught, and that doing so leads to better-quality groupwork.

Magician tip: A learning management system (LMS), such as Moodle or Google Classroom, can also be set up so that students can share and store their work for peer review. A magician teacher might assign students to a group that is reflected in the LMS setup that includes a discussion or board. Students upload their papers and use the discussion feature to provide specific feedback. Job tools that remind students what good feedback looks like can also be linked in the LMS.

MAKING THE GRADE (SCORING AND GRADING)

Our colleague, Magda Mostafa in the Department of Architecture at The American University in Cairo, recently noted that grades are a fairly poor business model, but they are the model we use. She has a point. Grades are a "familiar shore" (Ferguson, 2013, p. 195), even if they are flawed. Whether we teachers intend it or not, students come to think of themselves as "A" students or "C" students or "F" students. The scores that become a grade are more important than the learning that the grade is intended to represent. A grade may be intended as an incentive or reward, but it is also a threat, a threat that if the student doesn't do X well, a scarlet letter F will be forever fixed to his or her permanent record.

While learning how to "ungrade" a class is the subject for another book, we note here that grades and scores are not the same thing as assessment. Or at least they don't have to be. Remember Thomas's experience in seventh grade? The students in the class understood that what they learned was more important than the number of correct answers. An incorrect answer did not come with an additional penalty. Instead, an incorrect answer was a challenge, a puzzle to be solved. On the familiar shore of scores and letter grades, it is easy to mistake a grade or score for assessment *of*, *for*, and *as* learning. As we have pointed out, almost everything students do, create, or perform is a source of assessment information, but that need not mean that everything students do, create, or perform needs to go into the grade book.

CHAPTER 6

How Do I Improve My Use of Assessment Strategies?

There are many stories to tell when it comes to assessment. Your favorite one, most likely, is the story of individual student progress. But there are other stories. Let's zoom out and look at the big picture. For example, think a bit about the stories of your life and your family.

You have your own individual story and also the stories of your immediate family (partner, children, parents, and siblings) and your extended family (aunts, uncles, cousins, etc.). As these examples show, individual stories can also encompass larger units. We can think about assessment in the same way. You could talk about individual students, your class as a whole, and your school, district, and even state. Each assessment story uses assessments for different purposes and to communicate with different audiences.

As you begin thinking about how you can improve your use of assessment strategies, recall our examination of the purposes of assessment in Chapter 1. The first step is to consider what you are evaluating and who your audience is. Here is O'Connor's (2018) description of the four main purposes for assessment:

1. *Instructional uses:* To clarify learning goals, to indicate students' strengths and weaknesses, to learn about students' personal–social development, and to contribute to students' motivation.
2. *Communicative uses:* To inform parents or guardians about the learning program of the school and how well their children are achieving the intended learning goals.
3. *Administrative uses:* To include "determining promotion and graduation,

awarding honors, determining athletic eligibility, and reporting to other schools and prospective employers" (Gronlund & Linn, 1990).

4. *Guidance uses:* To help students make their educational and vocational plans realistically.

As we discuss the ways in which assessments are used and how to improve your use of assessment data, we refer to these purposes to make sense of the many kinds of assessment data available to you.

ASSESSMENT DECISIONS

As a teacher, you know that some things are under your control and others are not. You have students who arrive to class without breakfast and, in some cases, you can provide them with food via a school breakfast program. You can't give them a different home, however. The same is true for assessment. As you tell the story of student learning, you will be able to make many assessment decisions, especially those based in your own classroom. Some assessment decisions, however, will be made by policymakers. In this chapter, we focus on both kinds of assessments and what you can learn from each of them.

Distinguishing between Formative and Summative Assessments

Recall the two broad kinds of assessments we learned about in Chapters 2 and 3: formative and summative. Understanding these two categories will be helpful as we delve into state, district, and classroom assessments. To review how formative and summative assessments differ, Robert Stake provided a very rich illustration dealing with cooking (cited in Tomlinson & Moon, 2013). Think about making soup. (If you've never made soup before, think about making spaghetti sauce—or just some cooking shows you've seen on television.) When you're making soup, you may have a taste and think, "I'll add more salt." That's formative assessment. You're making decisions as you go based on a sample of your work. Using that principle in class-room assessment, if you are listening to a child read and hear him make miscues on the ending *-ing,* you might do a quick mini-lesson on words ending with that suffix. You are responding to a sample of student work through an assessment. Going back to our soup-making illustration, you might taste the soup and adjust the ingredients once or several times. As soon as you serve the soup to guests, however, you're done. You're not going to remove the soup, saying, "Oh, let me take it back and add more chicken stock." Instead, your guests will eat the soup, and most likely evaluate your cooking. That's summative assessment. In the same way, you might give your student an oral reading test that includes the suffix *-ing.* During the test, you'll be evaluating whether the student knows how to read words with this suffix. This is a summative assessment.

After finishing the summative assessment, you can revisit your teaching plan—or in the cooking example, your recipe. Summative assessment doesn't mean that you're finished with the concept once and for all. Let's say that you (and your guests) think the soup is superb. You might then decide that the recipe is exactly what you wanted. If, however, you're not entirely pleased with the recipe outcome, you might make notes to yourself, such as "add a second bay leaf," to try the next time. Summative assessments not only evaluate the outcome, they inform future instructional decisions. In the example of the test on oral reading using suffixes, the student may get all of them correct. If so, you probably won't revisit your instruction of this skill for the child in the near future. However, if the student makes several mistakes, you'll want to add more instruction on *-ing* to your lesson plans in your overall program.

Wise teacher tip: Errors crop up from time to time (see Figure 4.3 on p. 54 for more information about types of errors). But what happens when several students make the same error? Consider using error analysis to look for patterns among the errors. When several students miss item number 15 on the exam, that error is a clue that something went wrong. What went wrong is probably not the students' study habits. Instead, if many students missed the item, their attention was probably directed somewhere else, or perhaps the instruction did not address the content as fully as it might have. If many students are observed working on an essay but they do not write useful transitions between paragraphs or sections (Frey & Fisher, 2013), perhaps they need additional feedback. Notice how the procedure of error analysis is useful to students and to teachers. If many students do not correctly respond to an item on a summative assessment, the wise teacher does not penalize them. The source of the error probably lies somewhere else. If many students struggle with transitions in writing, the wise teacher, using formative assessment protocols, helps them one-on-one or in small groups or sometimes provides help to the whole class.

Trickster trap: What if students learned to analyze their own errors? Would they be better at avoiding them? Ask students to write in their journals or on an exit slip what they seem to consistently get wrong or what presents a repeated challenge. To do this well, students need to review the feedback they have been given and decide about where they might improve. Ask:

- What errors did I make?
- Why did I make them?
- How can I avoid or reduce these errors in the future?

What Do High-Stakes Assessments Mean to Me?

As stated earlier, you are not in control of all of the assessments that your students will take. For example, most of you will give students state tests. One purpose of these tests is to measure the level of student achievement on state content standards. Another purpose is to identify the percentage of students meeting performance standards. The data are used to compare school, district, and state achievement as a whole.

Assessments can serve multiple purposes, as we have noted. However, it is worth keeping in mind that there are compromises and trade-offs. The National Research Council (2001) noted how important it is to keep this fact in mind: "Often a single assessment is used for multiple purposes; in general, however, the more purposes a single assessment aims to serve, the more each purpose will be compromised" (p. 2).

Many of us might resist using high-stakes assessments and think that only individual student assessment should be our concern in the classroom. Understandably, student assessment and learning are the most important, but the compiled data of state assessments can provide you with important information about your program. Let's say, for example, that you found that students in general had good literal comprehension, but when it came to evaluative thinking they scored much lower. These data could signal your school to look closely at your overall program and identify how much it emphasizes critical thinking. A change to your program that incorporates more critical thinking could benefit all of your students. You can use the data from state tests in a way that benefits your students.

Policymakers use the information from state tests to determine whether a district or school is making progress as a whole. Teacher teams can also use this information, not to tell the story about individual progress, but to tell the story about the performance of their programs. Since all teachers are part of the overall picture of the school's achievement and reputation, they can use state tests to make decisions about program changes.

Often teachers don't think state assessments can help them, but they can. The purpose of state assessments is not to have teachers use them to tailor instruction to individual students, but rather to help them check how well their school's program is working. You might be thinking, "So what can I learn from them?" Let me (Susan) tell you a relevant story. I was working as a reading specialist in a district that had significantly more English learners and low-socioeconomic-status students than the other districts in the county. As part of a teaching team, we were quite happy with our students' achievement—that is, until the state decided to publish district results in the newspaper. When that happened, we found out that our school scored at the bottom of the district list. So, the first thing that state tests do is to compare your students' achievement to the standards and sometimes to other schools in your county, state, and the nation. The information is revealing. It's easy to be satisfied with your students' achievement, thinking that you've done all you can, when perhaps a reevaluation of your program of instruction is called for.

When we saw that our students scored at the bottom of the schools in the county, we first said, "But we have a bigger percentage of students living in poverty than the other schools do." We acknowledged the reality, but then we began looking at our program, especially our writing component. We found that many of our primary teachers weren't spending much time having students write. We met as a team and made some program changes. Then we asked teachers to review their writing instruction. I worked with individual teachers, encouraging them to be more intentional about how they taught writing. We implemented several changes, and within 2 years, our students were scoring near the top of the county. In this situation, the state test helped us improve our program and ultimately the learning of our students.

Standardized Tests: Norm-Referenced or Criterion-Referenced

State tests are summative assessments. They might be *norm-referenced* tests, in which scores are compared nationally, or they might be *criterion-referenced* tests, in which scores are compared to established literacy benchmarks or standards. Both kinds of tests are standardized.

As mentioned earlier, one of the state tests used is PARCC; another is the Smarter Balanced Assessment Consortium (SBAC). These state tests are designed to give consistent information on a state-by-state basis using the Common Core State Standards as the criterion. They are examples of *standardized tests,* which means that they have uniform procedures for scoring, administering, and interpreting the results. All students answer the same questions in the same way.

Standardized tests are created by a group of people who develop questions from a large bank of knowledge or from a set of standards. Proposed test questions are pilot-tested and then written so that they are within the content range. Methods for administering the tests are also developed and standardized. A scoring key and the method of scoring are provided. The test is administered over a large student sample and then developed into a score interpretation, which allows you to see how well your students have performed.

Standardized tests are generally of two types: *criterion-referenced* and *norm-referenced.* They serve different purposes, and therefore the way the items (questions) are constructed differs, as does the way we can interpret the results. In Figure 6.1, we have compared the two types, but please be aware that these are representative comparisons. A comprehensive review is beyond the scope of this book; however, several websites have useful information should you wish to explore the topic in greater depth. Criterion-referenced tests are standardized against specific criteria or standards, such as the Common Core State Standards (NGA & CCSSO,

	Criterion-referenced tests	Norm-referenced tests
Purpose	• Measures achievement against predetermined criteria, such as state standards or learning objectives. • May be used for pre- and posttesting.	• Measures achievement by comparing students' scores against a norming sample, or another group of students who were intended to represent those who would take the test. • Measures students relative to other students; thus, norm-referenced tests seek to highlight the differences between students. • May be used for diagnoses, such as placement on the autism spectrum.
What is tested	• Measures specific content knowledge expressed as learning objectives.	• Measure broad skills derived from a wide range of sources in the content domain being assessed.
Item construction	• To ensure reliability, each skill or disposition is tested multiple times (four times is common). • Items tested are written at a constant level of difficulty.	• Skills and dispositions are not usually tested multiple times because the test is designed to make broad distinctions relative to the content and the test-taking population. • Items vary in difficulty to increase the ability of the test to discriminate differences among the test takers.
Interpreting scores	• Individual students are compared against a predetermined standard. How the individual compares to other students is not relevant to the test result. • A student's score is usually expressed as a percentage. • Student achievement is provided for individual dispositions and skills measured against the standard.	• Individual students are compared with other students. • Scores are expressed as a percentile, quartile, stanine, or grade equivalent (but there are other types of scores). • Student achievement is provided for broad skill areas within a domain.

FIGURE 6.1. Criterion- and norm-referenced tests: What's the difference?

2010). Norm-referenced tests are standardized against a sample group intended to represent the whole population who have also taken the test.

Magician tip: Consult books and websites with useful information to learn more about standardized tests:

- Glossary of Education Reform (*www.edglossary.org*)
- Glossary of Standardized Testing Terms from ETS (*www.ets.org/understanding_testing/glossary*)
- *Standards for Educational and Psychological Testing* (American Educational Research Association, 2014; *https://amzn.to/2WzVIBh*)

Rebel tip: Check out the National Center for Fair and Open Testing (*www.fairtest.org*). This site advocates against standardized testing as a measure of student or teacher performance, among other things.

Percent, Percentage, and Percentile

Many people mistakenly believe the terms *percent, percentage,* and *percentile* are interchangeable, but they represent different mathematical information. We can start with the *cent* part of the word, which comes from Latin and means "one hundred." A percentage then is a ratio, so many of an item (such as correct answers) out of 100. If 52 students in your class of 100 are boys, then you have a 52% male population. Hopefully, you do not have 100 students in your classroom, and instead you have something like 36 or fewer. We can still use percentage to describe the ratio of boys to girls in the class by doing a little math. Since percentage is a ratio, we can represent the number of boys (or girls) as a fraction. Let's say we have 18 boys in the class of 36; we have 18/36. Divide the top by the bottom, multiply by 100 (notice the connection to "cent") and *voila!* Exactly 50% of your students are boys. A student who gets 45 out of 50 correct responses on a test would receive a score of 90%. Percentages make it possible to compare a fraction of something (e.g., correct responses) to the whole (all of the test items).

Percentiles are related to percentages, but they tell us something different. Whereas Mary's score of 86% on any given test stays the same, a percentile, as defined by statisticians, provides a way for us to rank Mary's score against her peers. Since Mary's percentile ranking is relative to other test takers, her percentile changes when the comparison group changes. The formula for calculating a percentile reports how well a student did by noting the number that falls below Mary's ranking. If Mary's ranking against a normative sample is in the 60th percentile, then 40% of the students in the norm group received scores higher than hers, and 60% received the same score or lower than she did. We can think of percentiles as a kind of percentage of percentages. The important thing for teachers to know is that percentages are absolute, but percentiles are not fixed and depend on the norming group. This is why it is possible for Mary to be in the 60th percentile with a score of 86%.

Sometimes test creators try to combine the best of the criterion and norm-referenced worlds into one test. Teachers trying to determine which kind of test information they have need to know that it is possible to have one test that contains criterion- and norm-referenced items.

CUT SCORES

A *cut score* is a choice made by test developers and administrators that indicates what they believe is an acceptable level of proficiency, or a passing score. Since cut scores are a choice, they are somewhat arbitrary. A cut score for a specified test in one school district may be different from a cut score in a neighboring district, even though the test is exactly the same. Keep reading to learn more about cut scores in Chapter 7.

State Tests and Classroom Assessments

Now let's compare state tests to classroom assessment. When standardized tests were developed, they were given to thousands of students to pilot-test items, to determine consistent directions, and to develop a scoring guide. Each time the test was given, the tester used the exact same directions so that the scores weren't influenced by the test administrator. If you think about this, you'll see that there could be variability in results just by how a teacher gives a test. Picture the different teachers in your school. Can you imagine some teachers adding information to the directions, possibly giving more time or assistance to students than other teachers? When this happens, results could vary, and the test wouldn't be as reliable and couldn't be used to compare students in different classrooms, districts, or states. In addition, interpreting test scores in a uniform way ensures a scoring guide that is the same for everyone. These factors increase the trustworthiness of the test scores, so you can comfortably use the results to examine your programs.

State tests aren't the only standardized tests you may know. Other standardized tests that you may be familiar with are intelligence tests (e.g., Stanford–Binet Intelligence Test), achievement tests (e.g., Iowa Test of Basic Skills), national tests (e.g., National Assessment of Educational Progress), international tests (e.g., Progress in International Reading Literacy Study, or PIRLS), and language proficiency tests (e.g., Test of English as a Foreign Language).

District Benchmark, Interim, or Common Assessments

Some districts have benchmark, interim, or common assessments. These assessments are typically decided at the district level, but sometimes these decisions are based on grant funding or on state policy. For example, many schools have used DIBELS as a reading fluency measure because they are required to be used to monitor progress. The purpose of these kinds of assessments is to measure the level of achievement toward state content standards. The data are typically used by district and teacher teams to determine program effectiveness and to identify program needs. They can also be used to identify students needing additional help and to monitor student progress. Teacher teams or individual teachers can use these data to plan instruction or interventions for groups of students or individual students. Sometimes district policymakers use these tests to gauge how much progress your school is making. For example, if 65% of your students in the past year made satisfactory progress in reading for the past 3 years, that trend indicates that your program is working, but if administrators have set a goal that 80% of the students make satisfactory progress, this different goal indicates that the program needs to be improved. Of course, you can't compare one year to the next because each year has different students. As you know, the abilities of students in any one year are different from one another. However, you can look at trends in the data. If the percentage of students making satisfactory progress is increasing, your program is becoming more effective.

Unlike classroom assessments, benchmark assessments need to be reliable and valid. Taking us back to the story metaphor, you know that when you talk about an experience you have a certain perspective, which informs the way you describe the events that happened. If someone else tells the story, the perspective and the story will be slightly different. When telling the story of different classrooms in a school, you want it to be told from the same perspective and with minimal differences. That means that you want everyone to be "on the same page."

We can achieve accuracy in assessment by making sure the assessment is reliable and valid. Reliability refers to the degree to which an assessment produces consistent results. Validity refers to how well a test measures what it is designed to measure.

The tricky thing is, of course, that you need to have realistic goals. Administrators who expect 100% of your students to meet benchmark goals in any given year are probably being unrealistic. But don't think of yourself as powerless. This is the time to educate yourself and other teachers about what reasonable expectations would be for your school or district and to develop a committee that would set goals that could be achieved.

In many circumstances, the district benchmark, interim, or common assessments are decided upon by groups that include teachers. As you think about what should be measured by a district benchmark assessment, ask these questions:

1. What literacy content should be measured across the school or district?
2. Does this assessment measure essential content?
3. How will the results be used to improve programs or individual achievement?
4. Is this assessment the best way to get this information?

DECIDING WHAT TO ASSESS

In this chapter, we have discussed how to improve your use of assessment strategies. As we think about this, we need to turn to what exactly you need to assess. Teaching is about making decisions and prioritizing. Deciding what to assess will depend on your students.

Assessment is part of the teaching–learning cycle. As you make every decision in the course of the cycle, you should be asking, "What should students know and be able to do to become proficient readers?" Wiggins and McTighe (2005) believe that making decisions about assessments needs to embody the standards and goals of instruction, not just measure outcomes. They offered the idea of "backward design" that begins with goals, then asks for the evidence that demonstrates learning, and finally plans instruction to meet the goals.

Assessment, therefore, should be intentional. As you think about how to better use assessment strategies, think about what skill needs to be assessed and then how you go about assessing that skill. Let's consider an example. I (Susan) was in a classroom recently, in which the teacher was assessing all of her students' oral reading fluency every 2 weeks using DIBELS. As you might guess, the process was taking a great deal of time, even with the assistance of support personnel. During the lunch break, we had an opportunity to talk about the reasons for using this assessment. The teacher was assessing every student because she thought it was expected. Coming from the Midwest, I shared a pithy statement: "You can only weigh a pig so many times, before realizing that you should feed it." After delving into her decision, we came up with a better assessment protocol. The teacher would only use DIBELS consistently to monitor the progress of students who had evidenced a weakness in oral reading fluency, and she would make sure that she was providing ongoing instruction in the skill more frequently than she assessed it.

STORIES FROM RESEARCH

Donald J. Leu, PhD, is Professor at the Neag School of Education at the University of Connecticut, where he directs the New Literacies Research Lab. Don is also a colleague, mentor, and friend of ours, and he has consistently influenced our research since we met him. Don and the New Literacies Research Lab always have something innovative in the pipeline to lead our thinking, and we are very pleased to introduce Don to you. We asked Don to tell us about the ORCA project: Online Research and Comprehension Assessment. ORCA addresses the need for assessments and resources for online inquiry and research in our schools. Read Don's response to learn more about ORCA and find the professional development resources that support it, all provided as a public service.[1]

What Is ORCA?

DONALD J. LEU

Central to our students' success in life will be the ability to conduct inquiry online in order to learn (Organisation for Economic Co-operation and Development [OECD], 2011). What does this process look like, and how might we determine our students' ability in this area so we can prepare appropriate instruction? The ORCA Project (*www.orca.uconn.edu*) recently developed eight authentic assessments to measure online inquiry skills in science (human body systems). A video describing these assessments is available at *https://youtu.be/aXxrR2wBR5Y*.

The assessments appear in two formats: ORCA–Multiple Choice (or ORCA–Closed) and ORCA–Simulation. In each format, students conduct online research about an important question in science, and their responses are

---

[1] This contribution is adapted from a post that originally appeared on *Literacy Beat*, April 17, 2016 (*https://literacybeat.com/2016/04/17/meet-the-influencer-don-leu*).

largely auto-scored. Both formats have demonstrated acceptably high levels of reliability and validity, although the ORCA–Simulation has demonstrated a 10% higher level of reliability compared to ORCA–Multiple Choice (see Leu et al., 2014).

Our research with representative state samples of 1,300 students in Maine and Connecticut shows that, on average, seventh graders only perform successfully on about half of the skills required in online research, suggesting that they are not fully prepared in this area. It also shows that students are especially weak in critical evaluation skills and communication skills (see Leu et al., 2015).

You are welcome to use these assessments for instruction, assessment, or professional development. A professional development module is also available.

ASSESSING THE ASSESSMENTS: QUALITY

Two critical criteria for fair assessment are *reliability* and *validity*. As stated earlier, reliability is a measure of the consistency of an assessment, and validity is a measure of how accurate the assessment is. In Chapter 7, we delve into this topic in greater detail. For now, we recommend that you use the checklist in Appendix C (pp. 172–173), *Assessing the Assessments: Quality*, as a way to begin thinking through just what it is that any teacher-created assessment (and maybe also assessments created by publishers and boards of education) measures, and how reliably it does so. Note that an assessment can be reliable but not valid; on the other hand, an instrument that is not valid cannot be reliable by definition.

To use the *Assessing the Assessments: Quality* tool, you will need an anchor to determine reliability. There are several ways to do this with teacher-made assessments. Give the same test to the same group of students at two different intervals (without intervening instruction). If the results are the same or very similar, that's reliable. Two different versions of the same test with items that are not exactly the same but reordered, or negative instead of positive responses (e.g., "The president of the United States in 1855 was Thomas Jefferson, true or false?" vs. "The president of the United States in 1803 was Thomas Jefferson, true or false?"), can also provide a measure of reliability. Split halves (say, odd-numbered and even-numbered questions) can test the internal consistency of the test by correlating the first and second halves against each other. If one half is low and the other is high, there is a problem.

Validity can be assessed in a variety of ways, some of which are better or more appropriate for the assessment type than others. For example, face validity is an assumption that an instrument (such as an exam) measures what it says it does. It is not very scientific, but it will do for many teacher-created exams. Similarly, a panel of experts on the content or process could decide that the exam or assessment instrument measures what it says it does. Criterion-referenced validity may be the most useful approach for teachers who work toward standards or some other standardized reference of ability. Sampling is another measure of validity that requires the assessment to cover the range of skills, attributes, or content knowledge that the subject requires.

We suggest using the following assessment principles in the context of your teaching:

- Make sure your objectives and standards are clear to your students. Write them down.
- Ensure that your assessments are aligned with the standards and objectives. Ask other faculty members to review your assessments before you use them.
- Ask students for their thoughts about what is confusing or troublesome.
- Compare your assessment instrument with others.
- Use item or error analysis to ensure fairness.

The scale used in *Assessing the Assessments: Quality* can be one that you and your colleagues devise. Of the five recommendations above, what most looks like a "five"? What most looks like a "one"? What examples from your assessment repertoire support your choices? Which examples from your colleagues' repertoires can you incorporate into yours? The discussion that ensues with your colleagues is likely to result in assessments that are more reliable, valid, and ultimately fairer.

A number of assessments ready made for diagnosis and progress monitoring are available. Here we present a compendium of compendia with links and descriptive information on various literacy-related assessments:

- SEDL at the American Institutes for Research provides a list of early literacy assessments (*www.sedl.org/reading/rad/chart.html*).
- The Center on Response to Intervention at the American Institutes for Research provides a list of screening instruments (*https://rti4success.org/resources/tools-charts/screening-tools-chart*).
- The Partnership for the Assessment of Readiness for College and Career (PARCC) website shares reading and writing evidence tables that you may find useful (*https://parcc-assessment.org/ela-literacy*).
- Literacy Leader provides a variety of assessment tools for reading (*www.literacyleader.com/node/318*).
- For English language learners, the Kansas Department of Education provides versions in multiple languages with the Home Language Survey and English language learner screening tools (*www.ksde.org/Agency/Division-of-Learning-Services/Special-Education-and-Title-Services/Title-Services/Title-III-State-ESOL*).

- Also for English language learners, Colorín Colorado maintains a list of sites by U.S. state, many of which include links to assessments for teachers of English language learners (*www.colorincolorado.org/ell-basics/state*).
- An analysis of reading inventories is found on Reading Rockets (*www.readingrockets.org/article/critical-analysis-eight-informal-reading-inventories*).
- The Reading and Writing Project at Columbia University provides resources for running records, assessing concepts of print, letter–sound identification, and high-frequency words (*https://readingandwritingproject.org/resources/assessments/running-records*).

STORIES FROM THE CLASSROOM

Robert Brewer is a seventh- and eighth-grade science teacher at Montera Middle School in the Oakland Unified School District in California. In this commentary, Robert describes for us his action research in designing and developing rubrics created by the students themselves.

Measuring On-Task Behavior and Results from Student-Created Self-Evaluation
Criteria for Summative Performance Tasks

ROBERT BREWER

BACKGROUND AND CONTEXT

My research on assessment techniques really began as a search for a better way to grade tests. I ended up with a method that improved classroom behavior during the test, that made students excited to take the test, and that increased learning. It even presented an opportunity for self-reflection. Science education has seen a huge paradigm shift in the last few years, although good science teaching has not changed. Students are tasked to apply their knowledge of scientific concepts in rigorous ways, but the assessment of that knowledge and standards have shifted from "Students know . . ." to "Students can . . .". The Next Generation Science Standards (NGSS Lead States, 2013) frame student mastery in "performance expectations" that challenge students' skills in doing science, not just knowing facts. To assess these skills, my fellow teachers in the Oakland Unified School District science department have been designing activities around the expectations. These activities often take the form of end-of-unit design challenges or problem-solving tasks. The tasks are rigorous multiple-day projects that require brainstorming, data analysis, modeling solutions, and reflection in both individual and group settings. We then developed rubrics to assess the projects and the various factors of the performance expectation, but in an effort to be thorough, the rubrics often turned out to be complicated, overly wordy, and confusing for teachers and students alike.

We also discovered an additional complication. Summative evaluation, a type of performance task, is new to some students in seventh- and eighth-grade classes. They are used to the "correct/incorrect" model of testing. Studying how students apply their knowledge in an unfamiliar situation is daunting and difficult. This confusion and uncertainty sometimes led students to shut down, veer off task, and become disruptive in the face of a high-stakes unit test.

EXPERIMENT

In looking for possible solutions to this problem, I came across research that suggested self-evaluation of assessments as a way to improve engagement and ownership of student learning. I also thought about taking the solution one step further and try to solve my rubric problem as well. I would have students grade their own submissions based on rubrics that they themselves had developed. Early in the year, I presented my teacher-created rubrics to students a few times before the performance task to familiarize them with the format. For the experimental task, I first presented the project, then we reviewed the content of the unit, then I guided students in the intervention groups through a process of writing their own evaluation criteria. The evaluation strands were inspired by the required expectations for that unit, but students had choices about which aspects they emphasized and how the performance levels (4, advanced; 3, meeting; 2, developing; 1, not meeting) were articulated. Control groups graded their own projects but did not go through the rubric writing process.

RESULTS

The results were well worth the experiment. Several different measurements suggested that students' enhanced involvement in the assessment of their work improved the test-taking process. The most profound results came from an observation protocol called BOSS (Behavioral Observation of Students in Schools). A fellow teacher observed my class and tallied students throughout the testing sessions in several different categories of on- and off-task behavior. The groups who had written their own rubrics seemed to have a better sense of the rigors and requirements of the project going into it. They showed a shorter lag time in getting started, fewer gaps in concentration over the course of the testing sessions, less disruptive off-task behavior, and greater levels of involvement from all team members in the group sessions. This last point may be one of the greatest successes. It is often difficult to get all students to participate equally in group tasks, especially if some do not feel prepared. The most frustrating part of my job as a teacher is how to work with students who feel insecure, then engage in disruptive behavior and interrupt the learning and performance of the entire class. This process really did seem to curtail this issue by adding an additional layer of preparation to the test.

Students in the intervention groups did score higher on average than the control groups, but there was also significantly less discrepancy between student self-evaluation scores and teacher scores. The students who wrote their own rubrics had a more accurate sense of their own performance, and I feel that involving them in the process sets them up to improve later.

The collected performance data already told a successful story, but the personal opinions of the students in pre- and posttest surveys also pointed out positive outcomes. Students indicated that they felt more prepared by writing the rubric, and even excited to take the test and to work together in their teams. Students in the control groups actually devalued the use of the rubric, saying that it did not help them prepare for the test, and were dissatisfied by the amount of work by their teammates. Students in the intervention groups felt that their teammates were more frequently on task and did their share of the work. It was really interesting to hear how students felt so dissatisfied and uninterested in the testing-as-usual situation.

Ultimately, I want my students not only to be successful, but also to believe they are successful. Involving them in more aspects of the assessment process gave them more control over their learning and more positive feelings about it in the end.

READABILITY AND PROFICIENCY

One aspect of assessing the assessment that literacy educators and their allies in other content areas should consider is readability and reading capacity (notice we don't write reading *ability*). All texts, be they books, newspaper articles, poems, or articles, demonstrate traits that make reading easier or more difficult, depending on the capacity of the reader to make sense of these traits. Readability scores are an attempt to guide teachers and their youthful readers to provide texts that students will find, well, readable.

 Wise teacher tip: Text levels have typically been addressed indirectly within past generations of standards documents. For example, a standard might describe fifth graders as needing to identify figurative language in "grade-level text," but *grade-level text* was not defined. Readability estimates were of some help; however, they are limited measures that cannot fully capture the complexity of a novel or expository text. By contrast,

Standard 10 of the CCSS (NGA & CCSSO, 2010) turns the spotlight of the English/Language Arts standards to ensure an increase in students' ability to comprehend more and more complex text during their school careers (Wolsey, Grisham, & Hiebert, 2012).

If students are to improve their proficiencies as readers, it is vitally important to know something about the complexity of the text (NGA & CCSSO, 2010, Appendix 10a) and how young readers make sense of text. Here we present some readability tools that will help you guide students to the texts they need and want to read.

- The SMOG generator at The University of Nottingham (*www.learningand-work.org.uk/SMOG-calculator/smogcalc.php*).
- Readable tools from WebFX Reviews provide multiple measures of readability for webpage and text you input (*www.webfx.com/tools/read-able*).
- Readability formulas also offer analysis of text using several measures of readability (*www.readabilityformulas.com*).

The Lexile framework from MetaMetrics is unique in that it generates a Lexile score for students and for books and other texts. The Lexile measure is shown as a number with an "L" after it—880L is 880 Lexile (MetaMetrics, 2019).[2] We take a closer look at the Lexile framework in Chapter 7.

 Trickster trap: Well-meaning teachers sometimes insist that students read books "at their level"—that is, whatever the students' grade level or reading ability score is should always match the books they read. In our experience, students are often willing to tackle texts that are beyond their abilities as assessed by readability and reading ability scores, and they often succeed with teacher guidance. Similarly, students who are reading well above the level of many of their grade-level peers often read the easy stuff from time to time. Student choice with teacher guidance can be a powerful tool.

STORIES FROM RESEARCH

Elfrieda H. Hiebert, PhD, is CEO and President of TextProject, Inc. (*www.textproject.org*), and a Research Associate at the University of California, Santa Cruz. Freddy has worked in the field of early reading acquisition for more than 40 years as a classroom teacher, teacher educator, and researcher. Her research, which addresses how fluency, vocabulary, and knowledge can be fostered through appropriate texts, has been published in numerous scholarly journals and books. In this commentary, she explains the importance

---

[2] For more information, see *https://lexile.com/educators/tools-to-support-reading-at-school/tools-to-determine-a-books-complexity/the-lexile-analyzer*.

of encouraging student choice, with teacher guidance, to inspire young readers and support their progress with challenging texts.[3]

A Text Complexity Toolkit for Teachers: Put a Priority on Teaching Students to Select Texts

ELFRIEDA H. HIEBERT

Reading always involves a reader and a text. In working to support their students' interactions with texts, teachers often wonder if they've provided appropriate texts. Are the levels appropriate? Too high? Too low? In response to these questions, there seems to be no shortage of systems that advise teachers about text complexity and suitability. The texts in most classrooms are organized by levels. All the texts at the same level are in one bin; texts at other levels are in other bins. If teachers work in a school that uses a particular independent reading program, texts are organized in yet another manner based on ATOS scores, a readability formula developed by Renaissance Learning. And, when it comes to state assessments, there is often yet another system for organizing texts—Lexile measures, a leveling tool developed by MetaMetrics.

Teachers no longer need to manually examine texts to determine complexity, since this information typically accompanies texts. An overall guided reading level (GRL) or Lexile score of a text gives a sense of where a text fits relative to thousands of other texts, but these designations do not inform teachers about the vocabulary recognition demands of texts. To increase their students' capacity with reading complex texts, teachers need information on vocabulary demands to understand which texts will aid in "growing" their students' reading and thinking. GRLs and Lexile scores provide an initial step in establishing the direction for instruction, but teachers' expertise will always be needed in determining the difficulty of texts for their students.

TEACH STUDENTS TO SELECT TEXTS

Teachers' guides include many recommended reading strategies. But rarely among the myriad strategies is anything said about the strategy of self-selection, which refers to students' ability to identify texts that they can comprehend. This strategy may be one of the most fundamental for a habit of lifelong reading. After all, once students have completed school, almost all of their reading as adults is self-selected. In classrooms where students' independent reading time is productive, lessons address how to choose texts (Manning, Lewis, & Lewis, 2010). Teachers

---

[3] This contribution is adapted from the article "Text Complexity Systems: A Teacher's Toolkit" (Hiebert, 2018), available at *http://textproject.org/text-matters.*

emphasize choices that include complexity of language and ideas and also students' interests and goals in reading.

In generations past, students were taught to apply the "five-finger" rule in choosing appropriate texts (Reutzel & Fawson, 2002). The strategy was to open a book randomly and to fold a finger for every unknown word. If, by the end of the sample, students had used up all of their fingers, the text was likely a challenging one. Recent digital analyses of texts give some credence to the five-finger rule. Middle grade to middle school texts typically have from 6 to 8 rare words per every 100 words (Hiebert, Goodwin, & Cervetti, 2018). If students can't figure out more than a handful of words in a sample of text, the text is likely to be challenging for independent reading.

An awareness of the challenge posed by new vocabulary in text is only one of the skills related to self-selection strategies. Consciously developing conceptual clusters of knowledge through reading is important. Recognizing that texts are the source for expanding one's knowledge and clarity about the areas in which one is gaining expertise are also critical aspects of independent reading. Students' interests quite naturally vary. One student might be particularly interested in stories of survival in adverse physical environments (e.g., *Hatchet* [Paulson, 1987]), while another student may be interested in the resiliency of characters in trying social environments (e.g., *Bud, Not Buddy* [Curtis, 2004]). Providing students with the tools to face the challenges of vocabulary, whether in narrative or informational text, will support their progress through increasingly complex texts for both school-based and pleasure reading.

CHAPTER 7

What Does This Assessment Information Mean to Me?

Have you ever been to a movie and had a debate afterward with your friends about what the movie meant? We certainly have. That's because movies (and stories) are subject to interpretation. The same holds true for certain kinds of assessment information. In this chapter we discuss how to interpret assessment data and how to make assessment data more meaningful.

In Chapter 6 we discussed high-stakes tests, including norm-referenced tests and criterion-referenced tests. Recall that intelligence tests, language proficiency tests, and most achievement tests are norm-referenced, and most state tests are criterion-referenced, with scoring tables that have been developed using norming groups. Most district and classroom assessments are criterion-referenced tests and are interpreted using scoring criteria, which can include rubrics.

Let's start with state tests. The first thing you need to know is whether your state test is norm-referenced or criterion-referenced. Your state might require a norm-referenced test, such as the Iowa Assessments, or it might require a criterion-referenced test, such as PARCC or SBAC. The following links will help you determine what tests are required in your state:

- State test list, grades 3–8: *http://ecs.force.com/mbdata/mbquestrt?rep=SUM1801*
- State test list, grades 9–12: *http://ecs.force.com/mbdata/mbquestrt?rep=SUM1802*

INTERPRETING NORM-REFERENCED ASSESSMENTS

Your state might require a norm-referenced test. If not, you still need to know how to interpret norm-referenced tests. Most tests that are given for special education referrals are norm-referenced. Some norm-referenced tests you might want to know are included in Figure 7.1.

Norm-referenced tests are designed to rank test takers on a distribution of scores that is described as a bell curve. A normal distribution is an arrangement of data in which most values cluster in the middle and the rest taper off symmetrically on both ends. The bell curve distribution is the distribution of scores that are produced after taking a random sample of the entire population. This explanation may seem counterintuitive to you, and there are certainly people who dispute this theory. Most teachers we know would never grade their students on a bell curve because it is inherently unfair to students. However, there are appropriate uses of the bell curve of normal distribution. Norm-referenced tests are scored and interpreted with the assumption that normal distribution clusters in the center, so let's keep going.

IQ Tests
- Stanford–Binet Intelligence Scales (SB5)
- Wechsler Adult Intelligence Scale (WAIS)
- Wechsler Intelligence Scale for Children (WISC)
- Wechsler Preschool and Primary Scale of Intelligence (WPPSI)
- Otis–Lennon School Ability Test
- Differential Ability Scales (DAS)
- Woodcock–Johnson Tests of Cognitive Abilities (WJ)

Achievement Tests
- Wechsler Individual Achievement Test (WIAT)
- Kaufman Test of Educational Achievement (KTEA)
- Woodcock–Johnson Tests of Achievement (WJ)
- Peabody Individual Achievement Test (PIAT-R)
- National Assessment of Educational Progress (NAEP)
- ACT (formerly American College Testing)
- California Achievement Test
- Iowa Assessments (formerly known as Iowa Test of Basic Skills)
- SAT (formerly Scholastic Aptitude Test)
- Preliminary SAT/National Merit Scholarship Qualifying Test (PSAT/NMSQT)
- STAR Early Literacy, STAR Math, and STAR Reading
- Stanford Achievement Test
- TerraNova
- WorkKeys
- Gates–MacGinitie Reading Tests (GMRT)
- Reading assessment database (*www.sedl.org/reading/rad/list.html*)
- Norm-referenced assessments (*www.sedl.org/reading/rad/chart.html#norm*)
- Criterion-referenced assessments (*www.sedl.org/reading/rad/chart.html#criterion*)

Language Proficiency Tests
- Test of English for International Communication (TOEIC)
- Test of English as a Foreign Language (TOEFL)
- International English Language Testing System (IELTS)
- Student Oral Language Observation Matrix (SOLOM) (*https://literacybeat.com/2016/01/07/solom*)

FIGURE 7.1. List of reading achievement tests.

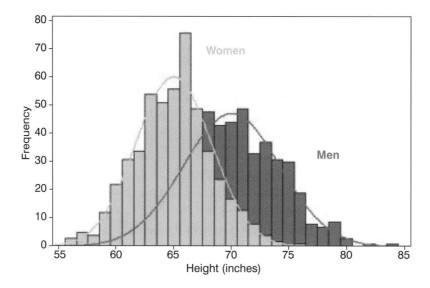

FIGURE 7.2. Distribution for height of men and women. Copyright © 2004–2019 Measuring Usability LLC. Reprinted by permission. Available at *www.usablestats.com/lessons/normal.*

Think about a topic that follows the principle of normal distribution: people's height, for example. If you measured the height of the entire U.S. population and plotted the results, you would come up with a graph resembling the bell shape of the normal distribution. If you plot the average, you would find that most people are similar to that height with an approximately equal number that are taller or shorter than average. In Figure 7.2, you will see that the normal distribution for the heights of men and women resembles a bell curve.

INTERPRETING NORM-REFERENCED DATA

The bell curve, or normal distribution, is the basis for interpreting data from norm-referenced tests. Norm-referenced data ranks test takers on a bell curve so that scores can be derived to compare students to the normal population. To accomplish this goal, test questions are designed to sample the content and to differentiate students from one another. (The test questions are not developed to determine how well students have achieved learning standards.) In other words, test takers develop questions that encompass content that students have not yet learned. These questions are chosen so that a small number of students excel and each test is difficult enough so that only a few students from a large population would get all items correct. These tests might seem hard to accept from a teacher's point of view. Just remember that they are developed for a large population, such as the entire country, not just the students in your class or school, so they have to account for a wide variety of achievement levels. Remember also that the bell curve represents the "average." When there is an exception, it is called an outlier. Outliers are often useful in determining the usefulness of the "norm." Figure 7.3 shows an example of a normal distribution curve with the kinds of scores you'll need to understand.

INTERPRETING NORM-REFERENCED SCORES

Now let's look at some student scores and discuss what they mean (see Figure 7.4). We first look at how the data are compared. Depending on the assessment, the data may be compared, for example, to a national norming group, a state norming group, similar-sized schools, and/or schools in urban areas. The reason it is important to compare data is because you need to know how the scores were derived. For example, your school might be located in a state that tends to have high achievement scores, let's say with a scale score average at 91, whereas the national average is 78. Remember that norm-referenced scores are comparative, so you need to be aware of what group your students are being compared to. If your students are being compared to the national norming group, a student who scores 78 would seem on target. If your students are being compared to a state norming group, the score would be below average. The scores you are interpreting would be different if the students are compared to a state norming group. In the case of this sample student shown in Figure 7.4, the scores are being compared to national norms.

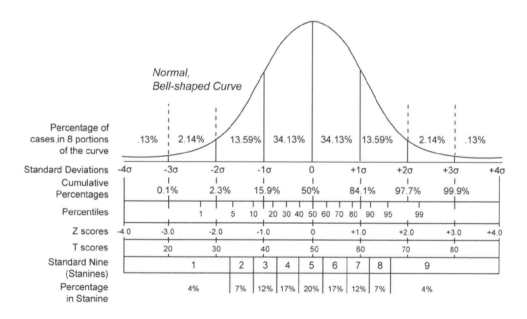

FIGURE 7.3. Example of a normal distribution curve with scores.

Name: *Sample Student*

Grade: *4*   National Comparison Group

Test	Number possible	Number correct	Scaled score	National percentile	Stanine	National NCE
Reading Total	114	81	613	65	6	58.1
Word Study Skills	30	17	604	55	5	52.6
Reading Vocabulary	30	22	603	54	5	52.1
Reading Comprehension	54	42	622	73	6	62.9

FIGURE 7.4. Student sample of achievement data. Stanford Achievement Test Series, Tenth Edition. Copyright SAT10 © 2019 NCS Pearson, Inc. Reproduced with permission. All rights reserved.

On the scoring sheet, there are four reading scores: total, word study, vocabulary, and comprehension. These four scores are common to many norm-referenced reading tests. The reading total score is helpful because it compares the student to how well he or she has scored in reading compared to a national sample. The subtests of word study, vocabulary, and comprehension can let you know whether the student scores better in any one subtest compared to the others. We describe what the reading total scores mean, and you can use that information as you look at the subtest scores.

The first two columns of data show the possible scores for each of the subtests and the number the student got correct (raw scores). The number correct was applied to the results of the norming group to get the scores in the remaining columns, which we describe next.

Scaled Score

A *scaled score* is a score that represents the raw score that is converted into a standard score according to the normal distribution. Scaled scores are useful because they can be compared. For example, the student in Figure 7.4 received 81 as a raw score for total reading. This raw score converts to a 613 as a scaled score. The raw score for word study was 17, with a scaled score of 604. You can see that these scaled scores are similar. As you interpret the results of this student's reading, you will notice that according to the scaled scores, reading comprehension is higher than the other subtests. In addition, you can use scaled scores to compare results from other norm-referenced tests since all scaled scores are compared to the normal distribution.

Percentiles

Percentile scores tell you something different. A percentile score does not compare the raw score to equal measures on the normal distribution scale; it shows how well the student did compared to the others in the norming group. A percentile score shows the percentage of students below that point. For example, the sample student scored in the 65th percentile (often written as 65%ile) in total reading. This score means that 65% of students scored below this student in total reading. The student scored in the 55th percentile in word study, which means that 55% of the students scored below this student in word study. The percentile score shows you how a student scored compared to others, in this case to the national norming group.

Stanine

The *stanine score* is a broad score that categorizes the scores on a nine-point scale. Typically, we consider stanines of 7–9 as above average, 4–6 as average, and 1–3 as below average. In the case of this student, the stanine of total reading and reading comprehension are 6. The word study and vocabulary scores are at stanine 5. What does this information mean? In broad strokes, the student is scoring high average in total reading and reading comprehension, and solidly average in word study and vocabulary. We often used stanine scores when talking to parents to show the general achievement level of their child.

Normal Curve Equivalent Score

The normal curve equivalent (NCE) score shows how the student did on a scale of 0–100. The NCE is different from a percentile score because the score uses equal values. That means the scores can be averaged. The student in this sample had a NCE of 58.1 for total reading. This score then could be used to average all of the students in the class to determine how well the entire group did.

Grade-Equivalent Scores

You might also come across tests that report grade-equivalent (GE) scores. For example, the test could report a GE of 5.2. Intuition may indicate that this score means fifth grade, second month. However, that's not what the score means. A GE shows where a student scores along a continuum. In our example, if a sixth-grade student earned a 5.0, that would mean that he or she had the same median score as a beginning fifth-grade student from the norming group, with an interpolation of 2 months. Here's another example. If a seventh-grade student scored a GE of 8.6, his or her raw score is similar to the raw score of a typical eighth-grade student at the end of their sixth month of school. The score does not mean that the seventh-grade student can read material that is at the eighth-grade level. What the score tells you is that the student is doing well. You can look at the scaled scored for a better interpretation of how the student is performing. The score sheet in Figure 7.4 does not report GEs because they are misleading and not very useful.

Score Bands

One more point needs to be mentioned in interpreting norm-referenced test data. Any test is a snapshot of learning, and you might be asking how accurate a test taken on any one day would be. You've all known what it's like to have a really bad (or really good) day. Think about a test you've taken, a race you've run, or a performance you've given. Sometimes the universe seems to be rooting for you, and everything goes according to plan. You're having a good day. On the other hand, let's say you're going to run a marathon, but you wake up the morning of the race with the flu. Not a good day for you! I'm sure you've noticed that your students have good and bad days as well. Students are taking these high-stakes tests on days that could be either good or bad for them.

Test reports often take this into consideration by reporting a *score band*. Score bands are based on the standard error of measurement, which estimates how repeated measures of a student on the same test tend to be distributed around a "true score." The score band is the confidence interval that gives the range of scores that would be considered accurate for students, taking into account that they have good and bad days and that no test is completely reliable. Figure 7.5 on page 136 is an example of a score band, with the associated Lexiles for each grade band presented as a range of possible levels. For example, a Lexile score of 846 should be interpreted as being within the range of 770–980 and the fourth- to fifth-grade band.

What Do These Scores Mean?

As you look at the sample student's scores, you can make some determinations. This student is doing above average compared to the national sample, but the student may not be achieving average scores compared to other students in your school. You need to look at the class scores to determine that. Furthermore, you can see that the student is doing better at reading comprehension than at word study and vocabulary. What do these results mean? You might consider adding more vocabulary instruction for this student (or for your class), but for most of us comprehension is a more important score than that in word study or vocabulary.

INTERPRETING CRITERION-REFERENCED DATA

Criterion-referenced scores are based on standards. You may ask, "Has my student met the standards?" The problem is that you don't actually know what score is necessary to satisfy the standards. When you are writing classroom assessments, you can decide what a passing grade is or what meets a standard or benchmark. For the state tests that are criterion-referenced, meeting the standard is usually calculated by a *cut score*.

A cut score is the point that is considered passing. You might also have scores that indicate not meeting standards, almost meeting standards, meeting standards, or exceeding standards. These scores could correlate to advanced, proficient, needs improvement, and unsatisfactory.

When you develop scoring criteria for a test you give, you are setting a cut score. For example, imagine that you are giving a test to a small group of students, and the scores are 98, 82, 79, 78, 77, 62, 55, and 41. We often look at a grading scale to determine grades, but we can also look at the score for meeting the criteria. Often we think of knowing 80% of the content as the standard. If we were not assigning grades, but using the test to measure knowledge of standards, only two students of the eight would pass. If the cut score was 75, five of the eight would pass. This is similar to the process that is used when determining the cut score for a criterion-referenced test.

Standard Setting

Cut scores are determined by a process referred to as *standard setting*. The cut scores set for state tests were most likely determined by subject-matter experts (SMEs). In many cases the experts review the test items to determine how closely the test items measure the criteria that increases the test's trustworthiness. The PARCC and SBAC tests were developed through a long process involving expert panels. After the tests were developed, individual states set their own cut scores using SMEs from the state. The state panel used a variety of criteria to set the cut score.

Cut scores might also be determined by correlating the scores to a norm-referenced test. For example, Sue was at an SMEs meeting to determine our state's cut score. The state test had been given to a large sample as the norming group. The experts then put the scores in order and looked at several cut scores. They used the cut scores to determine the percentage of students who would pass the test, and then compared that percentage to the NAEP test. The experts decided on the cut score that most closely aligned with the NAEP, and that score became the new cut score for the state. As you may have experienced, performance standards may change over time.

Cut scores can vary by state since each state determines its own cut score. For example, in Oregon, the SBAC reading cut score is 2,515, but in California, a neighboring state, the passing score is 2,581; in Washington, a state to the north, the passing score is 2,548. So, yes, a student could get a passing score in Oregon, but not receive a passing score in California or Washington. As you interpret criterion-referenced tests, you'll need to remember that the criterion for passing is determined by SMEs and is to be interpreted in the context of your state and district.

Lexile Scores

As we described in Chapter 6, the Lexile framework for reading is another example of a criterion-referenced test. You might see Lexile scores on your state test, on achievement tests, and on reading materials. That's because the Lexile framework provides two different kinds of scores: one for reader-based standards and one for performance-based standards. For example, in the sample score sheet in Figure 7.5, the student's Lexile score is 846. This is a reader-based score and reflects the student's reading ability when comparing this raw score to others in the sample. Grade levels have been attached to Lexile scores (see Figure 7.5). You can see that the student in the sample would be in the fourth- to fifth-grade band.

Text-Based Scores

The Lexile framework is interesting because it can be used not only to provide students with reading scores, but because it determines the reading-level scores of thousands of actual books so that you can match them with a student's reading ability. Lexile offers a couple of very helpful tools through their website (*https://lexile. com*). The first is a general Lexile Map that displays sample texts at the different grade-level bands.[1] You can take a look at the map and determine how accurate the group of books would be for your students or your grade level.

Grade level	Lexile range
K–1	*N/A*
2–3	450–790
4–5	770–980
6–8	955–1155
9–10	1080–1305
11–CCR (College and Career Ready)	1215–1355

FIGURE 7.5. Lexile levels according to the Common Core State Standards: Text Complexity (Appendix A).

---

[1]See *http://cdn.lexile.com/m/cms_page_media/135/Lexile%20Map_8.5x11_FINAL_Updated_May_2013%20(4). pdf.*

The second tool helps you determine the Lexile level for a specific book.[2] For example, let's say you were thinking of teaching *Through My Eyes: Ruby Bridges*. If you go to the Lexile Find a Book link, you would find that this book is rated at 860L. This is only a quantitative score. There are other factors that determine how difficult a book is to read, such as levels of meaning, the structure of the text, language conventionality and clarity, and knowledge demands. You can find out more about measuring text complexity at *www.corestandards.org/assets/Appendix_A.pdf*.

INTERPRETING SCREENING AND DIAGNOSTIC ASSESSMENTS

Informal reading inventories (IRIs) are individually administered diagnostic tests that help to determine a student's reading levels and instructional needs. IRIs can help assess a student's skills in word recognition, word meaning, reading fluency, and reading strategies and in listening, oral, and silent reading comprehension. You can use IRIs to place a student in a reading group, to screen for general reading difficulties, and to identify strengths and needs.

IRIs measure student reading compared to grade levels (not Lexiles) of texts according to three levels: independent, instructional, and frustration. The levels are often determined by the percentage of correct answers on the test (Betts, 1946). The independent level is the level at which the student can read without assistance. The student should score at least 95% correct on decoding skills and 90% on comprehension questions. The instructional level is the level at which the student can decode at least 90% of the words and answer at least 60% of the comprehension questions correctly. This is the level at which students can succeed with teacher instruction. Afflerbach (2018) compared this level of instruction to Vygotsky's (1978) zone of proximal development, or the area that students can learn best. The final level is the level of frustration, in which the student could not read the text successfully. Students who score below 89% on decoding questions and 50% on comprehension questions would most likely not be able to read the text.

What Do These Scores Mean?

It's important to consider that an IRI score is connected to how well the student can read text at a grade level. A student who scores at the instructional level of third grade benefits most from third-grade materials for instruction, no matter what grade level the student is actually in. For example, if you have a student in your sixth-grade class who is having difficulty reading, give that student an IRI, and the student scores at the instructional level of third grade, that result means he or she will learn best when given materials near that level.

---

[2] See *https://fab.lexile.com/book/details/9781419040290*.

STORIES FROM THE CLASSROOM

Douglas Fisher, PhD, and Nancy Frey, PhD, are professors at San Diego State University, and they also lead teachers at Health Sciences High and Middle College in San Diego. In their work with urban youth, they and the faculty at the high school wanted to know just how much impact they had in their teaching. This is their story.

Using Effect Sizes to Determine Impact and Adjust Learning Experiences

DOUGLAS FISHER AND NANCY FREY

A group of English teachers are gathered around a table, examining student work. They have identified students who struggled with a task and students who excelled. But one of them said, "We're having a hard time making sense of the unit. Was it effective? Did we make an impact?" This is not an uncommon challenge in professional learning community conversations. The focus is commonly on individual students who do not perform well, but rarely are teams encouraged to determine their impact on students as a whole and to consider adjustments to the entire learning experience. Luckily, this group of teachers sought out the answer to their question about impact and learned a great deal about instructional improvement in the process.

The unit under discussion focused on argument writing. Student results on the state assessment suggested that this was an area of need for many students. The teachers had collaboratively developed the unit, which included an initial assessment of students' writing for argumentation. They each engaged their students in a series of lessons focused on claims, evidence, and reasoning. The teachers modeled writing for students, demonstrating how to link claims to evidence. Peers provided each other with feedback based on the rubric the teachers had developed. The teachers collected writing samples from the students at the end of the unit of study and compared the results of the initial assessments with the postassessments. However, they didn't want to gauge only mastery—they were also interested in seeing progress. To do so, they used the progress and achievement tool, developed by the Visible Learning Plus team, to calculate the effect size and to visualize the data.[3]

This tool allows teachers to enter initial assessment and postassessment data and then calculate their impact on student learning. As is consistent with the Visible Learning database, the tool uses a statistical concept called an effect size, which is a measure of the magnitude of the impact of teaching. The larger the effect size, the bigger the impact. John Hattie (2009) used this tool to analyze meta-analyses, or aggregated studies, to identify what works best to accelerate

---

[3] See *www.visiblelearningplus.com/sites/default/files/Visible%20Learning%20Progress%20and%20achievement%20 tool_0.xlsm*.

students' learning. In Hattie's research, the average effect size was 0.40, which equates to approximately one year of learning for one year of schooling. Of course, teacher-created tools are not likely to have the same statistical power as published research, but teachers can use effect sizes to determine when they have had a meaningful impact on student learning.

The English teachers calculated the impact of their argument writing unit of study to be 0.73. They concluded that their efforts were effective. In addition to calculating an effect size, the tool produces a visual display of the data. The display includes four quadrants:

- The upper right, which indicates students who made good progress and who achieved well.
- The upper left, which indicates students who did not make progress but who achieved well.
- The lower right, which indicates students who made good progress but who did not yet achieve well.
- The lower left, which indicates students who did not make progress and who did not achieve well.

For the argumentative writing unit, the data visualization allowed the team to identify specific students who needed additional instruction and intervention to be successful. Overall, the teachers were pleased with their efforts to influence student learning relative to writing arguments. But they learned more about teaching when they next analyzed their efforts to improve students' public speaking skills.

The unit focused on improving students' public speaking skills. Lessons include focusing on prosody (e.g., intonation, pauses, emphasis); preparing drafts of speeches; and practicing and delivering speeches.

Six weeks into the unit, they collected data to make interim decisions about their impact of their efforts so far. They compared student performance on a writing rubric at the outset of the unit with the results obtained at the 6-week mark. The effect size was only 0.30. As one of the teachers noted, "They don't seem to be getting much better at this." As a result, they discussed changes that they could enact to ensure that students learned more. They agreed to implement a number of changes to the unit, including:

- Video analysis of effective and ineffective public speakers.
- Lessons about formal speeches sounding like reading, not friendly conversations.
- Written drafts of speeches that included an introduction, body, and conclusion.
- Anonymous peer review using computerized programs.

After another 6 weeks had passed, they collected additional data. When they compared the initial assessment and the 12-week data, the effect size was now 0.95. When they compared the 6-week and 12-week data, the effect size was 0.75. They concluded that the changes they made to the unit were useful and that they should implement the changes earlier in the unit the following year.

We believe that teachers want to have an impact on students' learning but have difficulty knowing whether they did or not. In too many cases, the impact is only determined on state tests, which may be too late in the teaching and learning cycle. These English teachers used the effect size calculator to monitor student learning and to make changes to the learning experience when the effect was not as high as desired. More important, the teachers had to identify the effect they were looking for because the Hattie hinge point of 0.40 may, or may not, represent sufficient learning when the time frames are reduced to a unit of study and when the reliability and validity of the assessments are unknown. Having said that, calculating effect sizes and visualizing the data allow teachers to engage in collaborative conversations with their peers and to adjust the learning environment when students do not make progress. To our thinking, these tools allow individual teachers, and teams of teachers, to make decisions about their next steps in the learning process.

INTERPRETING CLASSROOM ASSESSMENTS

Rubrics and Scoring Criteria

Many of you use rubrics to score program and classroom assessments. A rubric is a type of scoring guide used to assess performance against a set of scoring criteria with descriptions of levels of performance. You may wish to review the section on rubrics in Chapter 5.

Bias in Testing

You come across examples of "research" all the time. For instance, think of a television commercial that claims "In a clinical study, 78% of people surveyed found that this pillow improved their sleep." Although on face value this statement might sound impressive, there are obvious issues with this statement—for example: "How many people were surveyed?"; "Did these people have a vested interest in the company?"; "How do you measure 'improved sleep'?"; "What were the characteristics of the people surveyed that might affect sleep?" These kinds of questions make the claim unsubstantiated.

Statistical Bias

When educational tests are developed, they are tested for statistical bias. The questions are tested for clarity, and items are reviewed for obvious bias. The tests are then given to representative populations, and the results are compared to normal distribution graphs. However, many forms of bias cannot be removed because there are cultural assumptions built into the test and not all underlying bias in the test's form and content are addressed.

Cultural Bias

Cultural bias means that certain cultures and minority groups are at a disadvantage when taking a test. When a test does not evaluate a student's actual knowledge or includes ideas that are tied to a culture, it can be considered culturally biased. Bias is closely related to fairness. Do the tests unfairly advantage certain groups of students? If so, that test could be considered biased. Here's an example of a test question that could be considered unfair for many people.

> *Directions:* What is the missing word of this analogy?
>
> Runner is to marathon as _____ is to regatta.

The answer is *oarsman.* Did you get it correct? This question requires the cultural knowledge of rowing, which is a sport that is concentrated in a few areas of the United States and is typically, but not always, popular with wealthy people. When I (Susan) was a reading specialist in a poor suburban school, the writing test had the prompt: Compare urban life to rural life. My students were stumped. They had no conception of urban life, and even though they lived 14 miles from a large urban center, they had never visited the city. Neither had they any substantial knowledge of rural life. They had never traveled to a farming area and had no idea what life in a rural community would be like. Even if these third graders knew the vocabulary terms *urban* and *rural,* they had no concept of how to compare the two lifestyles. I'm sure you have experienced many other examples of test questions that were outside the experience of your students. These tests could be considered culturally biased.

If you want to experience how it feels to take a culturally specific test, you might want to take the *Original Australian Intelligence Test,* which was developed in 1971 to illustrate how cultural knowledge makes a difference in how you might score on a test. Try it out, and you'll be able to experience how many of your students feel when they take standardized tests.[4]

---

[4]See *www.wilderdom.com/personality/intelligenceOriginalAustralian.html.*

Opportunity Gap Instead of Achievement Gap

There is one more subject we want to discuss as you interpret your students' test scores. As you look at state scores, you will most likely observe that they are reported by gender and ethnic groups. If you compare the scores of the groups, you might find a discrepancy in educational outcomes, which has been termed an "achievement gap." According to Gay (2010), "achievement gaps in the quality of experiences and outcomes at all levels of U.S. public education is relentless and extensive" (p. xvii). The achievement gap was brought to the public's attention when No Child Left Behind legislation required states to disaggregate data based on subgroups. Once the achievement gap became publicized, scholars began to expand the conversation by asking for reasons for the differences in test scores (see Ladson-Billings, 2006, 2013). Looking at achievement solely through the lens of test scores emphasized a symptom of a problem in education. In trying to identify the unequal opportunities that resulted in the achievement gap, researchers (Milner, 2015; Welner & Carter, 2013) highlighted the complex causes for the differences in test scores and referred to them as the *opportunity gap.*

According to Welner and Carter (2013), "the 'opportunity gap' frame . . . shifts our attention from outcomes to inputs—to the deficiencies in the foundational components of societies, schools, and communities that produce significant differences in education—and ultimately socioeconomic—outcomes" (p. 3). One of the reasons to think about test score differences through the lens of the opportunity gap is to avoid a "deficit gaze." One of the consequences of a deficit gaze is that teachers do not look for instructional ideas that could benefit all students and that ignore the cultural wealth that students bring with them to class (Yasso, 2005). So, your students' scores could also be signaling that they need more focused instruction in some areas to reduce the opportunity gap that exists between groups.

Reducing the Impact of Testing Bias

Although this chapter has primarily discussed how to interpret test scores, we would be remiss if we didn't also encourage you to reduce the impact of testing bias. As you look at the results of standardized tests, consider the possibility of cultural bias. As you interpret test scores, we think it best to consider what Kim and Zabelina (2015) had to say: "Standardized tests intend to measure intelligence and general knowledge, but they are normed based on the knowledge and values of the majority groups, which can create bias against minority groups." As you look at the scores of students who are not in majority groups, you might think about the score bands and believe that your student's true score is at the highest part of the score band and could be potentially more accurate when accounting for cultural bias.

As you make classroom or programmatic decisions as a result of these standardized tests, also consider the possibility of opportunity gaps. If you have English learners, Hernandez (1994) suggest that you do the following:

- Increase your knowledge/awareness of your students' cultural and linguistic background.
- Determine the level of your students' acculturation.
- Control cultural variables.
- Determine the language or languages used in testing.
- Use interpreters when you can to get a more accurate picture of the students' achievement.

CHAPTER 8

How Do I Communicate with Others about Assessment?

Now that you're comfortable (we hope!) with the kinds of assessments students take and how to interpret the data, you can think about how to communicate to other stakeholders about the assessment results. Before we begin discussing assessment results, we need to consider who has the right to assessment data and how to protect a student's privacy. Let's turn now to ethical concerns about assessment in general.

ETHICAL USE OF ASSESSMENT DATA

The purpose of standardized tests is to give an accurate measure of students' knowledge and skills. Standardized tests measure a domain of knowledge, which means that the questions on the test are a sample of the concepts being tested. These tests are not the same as quizzes, which measure a small amount of specific knowledge. As a teacher, you want to expose students to the broad range of knowledge, and trust that your students' test scores will be accurate. It is not ethical to offer instruction so that students increase short-term learning and test scores only to forget what they have learned right after the test. Not only is it unethical, but it's also unfair to teach students something only so they can have a high test score.

You don't want scores that are artificially high or low. You want your students to achieve as high a score as they can, but when are you "teaching to the test"? When you think about what is ethical or unethical, you can mostly use common sense. So, it's ethical to teach the content that would appear on a test. For example, you can teach students how to find the main idea in a paragraph because this is a skill that you would normally teach, but you can't use the same paragraphs that are found on the test. You can review skills, strategies, and concepts that you taught previously, but it would be unethical to only review skills you think are on the test. You can also familiarize students with the format of a test. For example, if your students have not worked with multiple-choice test items in your class, you can give them practice tests using this format, so they are familiar with how to answer the questions. When students understand the test format, they have the potential to get a score that more accurately represents their actual knowledge.

It is not ethical to teach in a way that would cause students to receive scores that do not match their actual knowledge. It would be unethical to give students any assistance on the test. For example, if there is a word on the test that is unfamiliar to your students, you cannot pronounce it for them. Most norm-referenced tests are copyrighted. Therefore, you also can't copy or reproduce any of the test questions. And, of course, you can't coach students during the test or change test answers. That would be cheating. A final unethical practice is to exclude any eligible student from taking the test in order to try to improve your class or school average score. Remember, you want to know how well your students have learned, and you want the test results to be as accurate as possible. Low scores can be as informative as high scores.

THE FAMILY EDUCATIONAL RIGHTS AND PRIVACY ACT OF 1974

The Family Educational Rights and Privacy Act of 1974 (FERPA) is federal legislation that protects the privacy of students' personally identifiable information and applies to all educational institutions that receive federal funding.[1] The law details what information can be shared without violating confidentiality and what information can only be shared with the students and parents. Some information that would be in the public record can also be released. Examples include a student's name, home address, email address, place of birth, or grade in school. However, even though this information can be made public under the law, many districts may not allow it, and most teachers do not give out this information without a reason.

The purpose of FERPA is to protect the privacy of students and to safeguard the confidentiality of their educational records. FERPA also allows students and parents access to educational records. That means that parents have the right to see their child's records—and so do students. Files, documents, grades, test results, and written comments about a student's performance are all records that are available to parents and students. A teacher does not have to disclose individual records that are written for their personal use and are not part of a student's educational record. For example, notes written about a student that are shared with a substitute

---

[1] You can find more detailed information about FERPA at *www.fordham.edu/download/downloads/id/1850/09_-_dos_and_donts_for_teachers.pdf*.

teacher do not need to be shown to parents if the notes are not part of the student's educational record.

As a teacher, you must safeguard your students' educational results; they are private unless a student's consent is obtained. You cannot post test scores on a bulletin board or ask another student to pass out graded papers. You cannot stack graded papers in a box for students to go through and collect. You cannot post grades on the Internet. You also can't send grades by email. You can have students assess each other's work while they are learning, but once a paper is graded by the teacher, the paper can't be shared with anyone other than the student or parent.

There are a few exceptions to this privacy rule. Sharing a student's test scores with another teacher on your team would be allowed. However, you couldn't just tell all of the teachers at lunch how a student scored on a test, since not every teacher would have a legitimate interest in knowing that information. You can also disclose information if it is necessary to protect the safety and health of the student or if the student is transferring to another school or needs the information for financial aid.

As you think about who has the right to student assessment information, it's best to ask yourself whether you're revealing private information to someone who does not need it to benefit the student. If you are unsure, ask an administrator.

STORIES FROM RESEARCH

Ibrahim Karkouti, EdD, teaches international and comparative education courses to under-graduates and graduate students at the American University in Cairo. He specializes in organizational leadership and school effectiveness. Knowing how and why to evaluate pro-grams is an important part of being assessment literate. Here, Ibrahim explains the process of evaluating a school's culture and its evaluation processes, and he provides recommen-dations based on his case study of an international school in Qatar.

Program Evaluation

IBRAHIM KARKOUTI

Human resources highlights the relationship between employees and organiza-tions. According to Bolman and Deal (2008), the human resource frame views people as an organization's most valuable asset. Despite this fact, many organiza-tions "exploit people—chew them up and spit them out" (p. 117). Today, many organizations view employees as objects to be exploited, and consider that workers have no rights beyond a paycheck. Although such assumptions have forced many corporations out of business, they are still widely employed in the workplace. Using Bolman and Deal's human resource frame as a lens, this section examines one international school's ability to attain its mission. Specifically, this section analyzes the New International School's (NIS) human resource frame in an effort to understand its impact on faculty performance and the school's overall culture.

How Do I Communicate with Others about Assessment?   147

According to Bolman and Deal (2008), organizations prosper when they create a good fit between employer and employee that benefits both. On the one hand, employees excel at work when they are able to apply their skills, to express their sense of self, and to fulfill their financial and lifestyle needs. On the other hand, organizations thrive through getting the talent and the energy they need to succeed. When the fit between individuals and the system is poor, one party or both suffer. In summary, the human resource frame "centers on what organizations and people do to and for one another" (p. 117).

Bolman and Deal (2008) explain that the human resource frame focuses on the interdependence and the interrelationship between employees and their organizations. In addition to bolstering employees' performance and productivity, organizations that respond to the needs of both employees and customers attract the best talents who are motivated to do a good job. In conclusion, the human resources frame aims to achieve mutual benefits for both employees and employers. When employees are exploited, organizations suffer because employees retaliate and work against the organization's purposes. Conversely, when employees collaborate and unite their efforts, both employees and organizations attain their needs.

Before beginning to analyze NIS's human resource frame, I would like to briefly discuss an aspect of the Qatari labor law that governs foreign employees' working conditions in Qatar.

The sponsorship, or the *kafala*, system in Qatar and most Arab Gulf States negates the basic human needs that Maslow (as cited by Bolman and Deal, 2008) identified. According to Scott (2013), a sponsorship (*kafala*) system links every expat employee to a single employer. This arrangement means that employers are the ones who decide when an employee is allowed to leave the country. Montague (2013) pointed out that Human Rights Watch and the International Trade Union Confederation described the sponsorship system as a form of modern slavery. In addition, the sponsorship system entails using an exit visa that prevents employees from traveling without their employer's official consent.

Specifically, the sponsorship system requires expat employees to obtain their employer's official approval prior to changing their jobs, leaving the country, getting a driver's license, renting a house, or opening a checking account (Khatri, 2012). In summary, the human resource frame does not apply at a great number of workplaces in Qatar because the Qatari government still upholds a system that deprives employees of their basic human rights.

SCHOOL BACKGROUND

Located in Qatar, NIS is a K–12 international school that follows the American system. NIS enrolls more than 1,800 students of diverse nationalities and backgrounds. English is the primary language of instruction, and the total number of employees, including faculty and staff, is 211. Faculty and student bodies are diverse and represent over 42 countries. Around 86% of faculty and staff hold bachelor's degrees, and 5% hold masters and doctorate degrees.

NIS HUMAN RESOURCE FRAME ANALYSIS

Given my observations and field interviews with teachers, it became evident that the majority of NIS seniors (i.e., department heads and subject coordinators) manage their departments and instruct their subordinates through employing McGregor's (1960) soft version of Theory X. That is, subject coordinators and department heads micromanage daily tasks because they lack confidence in faculty members' expertise. This mechanism has turned the whole school into militant units, in which faculty and staff who share common interests form alliances that antagonize and alienate other colleagues.

The formation of these units aligns with Argyris and Schon's (1996) Model I theory of action. The model suggests that employees view their organizations as dangerous places when their needs are not met. As a result, they form alliances to protect themselves and their interests from what they perceive as threatening. The strained relationships between faculty members and their supervisors at NIS have shortchanged many educational initiatives, including integrating technology into instruction. In summary, organizations that utilize this model suffer from strained relationships among workers, resistive behaviors, and deterioration in decision making.

NIS faculty members' basic human needs are not fulfilled owing to the national rules and regulations that govern foreign employees. According to McGregor (1960), the deprivation of both physiological and higher-level needs has behavioral consequences. The lack of independence, free association with other colleagues, and safety leads to hostility, passivity, and resistance. This notion explains why many faculty members resisted integrating technology into their instruction.

NIS's faculty and staff escape their frustration at work through physiological withdrawal. Due to the high rate of chronic absenteeism and tardiness, NIS's principal has had to hire two substitute teachers for each department in order to avoid disrupting the educational curriculum.

Few subject coordinators and department heads advocate McGregor's (1960) Theory Y. Instead of emphasizing the tight control mechanisms of Theory X, they align their teachers' interests with the school's organizational purposes. Furthermore, they resolve conflicts through employing the situational leadership model (Hersey, Blanchard, & Johnson, 2001), which allows subject coordinators and department heads to adjust their leadership behavior according to the situation they are facing. The academic departments that highlight such effective leadership behaviors are the most productive, effective, and efficient in terms of accomplishing NIS's mission statement.

NIS Decision-Making Process

At NIS, decision making, for the most part, is the product of collaboration and coordination between department heads and the school principal. Faculty are not included in the process, and their contributions are disregarded given the school's vertical organizational structure. Once the school principal approves a decision, the department heads hand it down to their subordinates (i.e., subject coordinators), who supervise the implementation process.

Performance Evaluation

NIS's subject coordinators and department heads are solely in charge of supervising and evaluating faculty performance. They assess faculty progress in attaining both the school vision and mission through checking their weekly lesson preparations, conducting classroom observations, holding weekly meetings, and analyzing parents' feedback. Interestingly enough, the school's human resources department does not employ any form of professional appraisal systems. According to Graham and Bennett (1998), professional appraisal can be classified into two categories: (1) performance reviews and (2) potential reviews. Performance reviews analyze employees' achievements and failures and include a plan to improve their performance in the future. Potential reviews evaluate employees' eligibility for promotion and professional development.

Action research is defined by Creswell (2005) as a "systematic procedure done by teachers (or groups in an educational setting) to gather information about, and subsequently improve, the ways their particular educational setting operates, their teaching, and their student learning" (p. 550). School administrators identify educational shortcomings through examining students' formative and summative test scores. In order to overcome teaching challenges, department heads rely on peer-coaching and coteaching strategies. Department heads rarely use action research in solving school problems due to the lack of cooperation and collaboration between individuals and groups.

Recommended Solutions

The best way to improve human resource management at NIS is to develop and implement a human resources philosophy that values faculty and staff contributions in attaining the school's vision and mission. Informed by Bolman and Deal's (2008) framework, Figure 8.1 offers recommendations for future practice. These recommendations can help NIS educational leaders reform the school's organizational and human resources structure.

Human resource principle	Description
Build and implement an HR strategy.	• Develop a shared philosophy for managing people. • Train faculty and staff on how to implement the philosophy.
Hire the right people.	• Select creative and talented prospective employees.
Keep them.	• Reward well, protect jobs, promote from within, and share the wealth.
Invest in them.	• Create professional development opportunities.
Promote diversity.	• Stress the importance of having diversified social and educational backgrounds in achieving the organizational purposes.
Empower them.	• Foster self-managing teams. • Encourage autonomy and participation.

FIGURE 8.1. Basic human resource strategies.

COMMUNICATING ASSESSMENT INFORMATION

Now that we've discussed ethical uses of assessment data, we can think about how to communicate that data to administrators, policymakers, other teachers, parents, and students. While it is important to document what students know and can do throughout the instruction and assessment cycle, record keeping is of particular importance when communicating with parents. Evidence of learning demonstrates what parents and caregivers need to know about the progress of the children in their care. What examples can you provide of the ways you record student progress and achievements? Use the form in Appendix D, *Assessing the Assessments: Documenting and Record Keeping* (pp. 174–175), to review your process for organizing and storing assessment information.

Administrators and Policymakers

As we discussed earlier in this book, administrators and policymakers receive assessment results, which most likely is compiled information about the students of each teacher in the district, class assessment information, and school or district information. You will not personally communicate the assessment results, but you might be in meetings in which you discuss how to respond to them. As you think about the role of administrators and policymakers in making assessment decisions, remember that they will not be using assessment data to consider individual student progress, but to evaluate the success of school programs and curricula and to make decisions about how they can be improved.

Therefore, your first course of action is to check online and look at your school or district's state report card. States have the flexibility to report achievement data in different ways, using the guidelines from the Every Student Succeeds Act (ESSA).[2] You need to be familiar with how your state reports the data that administrators and policymakers use to make decisions, and then think about what else these stakeholders need to know as part of the process. Here is where your perspective as a teacher or teacher leader can help round out their views as they make decisions.

Let's use the example of the Ohio State Report Card (*https://reportcard.education.ohio.gov*). In this case, schools and districts are graded on the categories of achievement, progress, gap closing, graduation rate, improving at-risk K–3 readers, and prepared for success. Under each of these categories, you can click on the tab "View more data." For graduation rate, you'll find the district's score; the "grading scale for the score"; and comparisons between the district, state, and a similar district. There are also trend data. You can look at the district overview to find out district details, including the grades for each of the schools in the district.

As you analyze your school or district's state report card, and if you have the opportunity to meet with administrators or policymakers, to write an opinion piece for the newspaper, or to speak at a local meeting, it's important to keep in mind what these tests measure and what this information might mean for your school and your students. First, try not to be defensive. If you receive a "C–" in achievement, think clearly about what this score means. First, look at the exact definition and how you were graded. In this case, achievement is defined as "student performance on state tests met established thresholds and how well students performed on tests overall." What does this definition mean? According to the calculations, students are performing slightly below average according to the established threshold. As you communicate with administrators and policymakers, we don't recommend that you attack or criticize their decisions. You might, however, ask some questions, such as "How confident are you in the thresholds?" and "In what ways do these grades (or scores) represent the real achievement of our students?"

If your class scores are relatively low, you can use the information as an opportunity to educate administrators and policymakers about your instructional needs. For example, this could be the perfect time to discuss class size, new curriculum materials, or additional teaching assistants. It's important to remember that a low score is not a reflection on your teaching, as much as one part of the story of student learning. As you communicate with these stakeholders, you might focus on other parts of the story, such as improving student attitudes toward reading, increased parental involvement, or other needs. When you voice your concerns, it can sometimes be helpful to tell an anonymous anecdote about an individual student to clarify your points.

---

[2] For the ESSA guidelines, see *www2.ed.gov/policy/elsec/leg/essa/essastatereportcard.pdf.*

Other Teachers

There are situations in which you will share a student's assessment results with other teachers, such as in team meetings, individualized education plan (IEP) meetings, and in informal conversations. You may be discussing assessment to evaluate the curriculum or to make changes to instruction or you may discuss assessment results about an individual student.

Evaluating Curriculum and Instruction

Assessment results can help teacher teams make decisions about curriculum. As you look at the assessment results of your class, you'll want to look at the components of the scores and even do an item analysis. Many tests provide a breakdown of how students scored on each item. If you have this information, you can look for areas in which your students did well or did poorly. For example, when Sue was a reading specialist, we met in grade-level teams to discuss achievement data. In the fourth-grade meeting, we noticed that students scored very low on identifying the main idea or topic of a paragraph. Even though this skill is a tough one for all grade levels, we determined that it was an important skill for reading comprehension and that we should increase the time spent on identifying main ideas and make it a priority of our reading program. We all discussed instructional approaches and decided that we would informally make this adjustment to our curriculum for the rest of the year and that we would formally amend our curriculum for the following year.

Discussing a Student's Progress

You might also discuss a student's progress in a team or an IEP meeting. You'll want to bring the student's assessment data from state tests or other norm-referenced tests, which are typically compared to national norms. As you discuss the student's progress, you might also consider discussing classroom data. For example, if Kaitlin scored in the 45th percentile on total reading, it can be helpful to contextualize the score. As you learned in Chapters 6 and 7, a 45%ile score means that Kaitlin scored better than the students in the national sample. You might compare this score to your class average. Perhaps your class average is 48%ile, which would mean that Kaitlin scored slightly below average in your class. If your class average, however, is 62%ile, Kaitlin scored significantly lower than most of the students in your class and needs additional support. Your role in these meetings is to present the student's score within the broader story of the student and of class achievement. As the student's teacher, you have additional information that can make sense of assessment data. As the teacher, you'll be expected to bring the assessment results to the table and also additional information that could be used to make a plan to help the student progress.

Parents

All parents have stories about their children, and these stories sometimes include their child's performance at school. When communicating with parents, you will most likely encounter some who have preconceived notions and beliefs about their child. Sometimes their beliefs are overly positive, and sometimes they are overly negative. Results that differ from their beliefs are hard to hear and harder to comprehend. You see a student, while a parent sees an entire person; perspective makes a difference. It's important to remember that, although the child's literacy progress is your responsibility, the child is much more than his or her test scores, and that's the perspective the parents may have as they hear critical comments about their child.

As you talk with parents, then, endeavor to be honest and to help them understand the most accurate picture of their child's achievement. It's easy to be so vague that parents leave conversations about assessment results with a distorted view of their child's achievement. Remember that assessment results tell us as accurately as possible how the student is achieving as measured by a particular test. You can help them understand the scores with that perspective.

Official Reports from Norm-Referenced and State Assessments

Parents have access to their child's assessment data. Most states have "report cards" that detail a student's scores on a state assessment. Some communications to parents, as in Kaitlin's example, show where the student's score falls on a continuum. After looking at the data, parents may have questions. We discussed how to interpret assessment results in Chapter 7. Our experiences working with parents suggest that you help them think through three main points:

1. Make sure that parents understand what exactly the assessment was measuring. For example, a state reading test that measures reading comprehension may not evaluate phonics skills. It's important to remind parents that the test does not measure every aspect of a student's literacy. There are many components of learning, and tests assess only some of them.
2. Make sure that parents understand score bands and that the score their child received could be higher or lower. Some parents believe too strongly in a single score. Help them understand that their child's score is "plus or minus" the number they were given.
3. If the test is norm-referenced, explain the two types of scores—one based on standard deviations and one on percentiles—to give parents a realistic picture of their student's progress. I always like to also give parents a percentile score because many can relate to a score that compares people. For example, if their child scored 78%ile, it means that out of 100 students

at that grade level, the child scored better than 78 of every 100 students. If the assessment was criterion-referenced, as are many state scores, the child's score will be evaluated on whether it met the criteria or benchmark expected for students at that grade level.

How Can Children Improve Their Test Scores?

When you're discussing test results with parents, they may ask you how they can help to improve their child's test scores. As you answer this question, make sure that you help parents understand that it will be more beneficial for their child to improve his or her understanding of broad concepts rather than working on specific components of the test. For example, if the child scored low in word study, you could suggest a generic workbook at grade level that the child could complete for extra practice. If the child scores low on vocabulary, you might provide parents with a grade-level vocabulary list and have them work with the child to learn the words in actual reading contexts. If the child scores low on reading comprehension, you should encourage parents to give the child opportunities to read at-level interesting books. If the parent wants to employ a tutor, you should give these suggestions to the tutor. It is never appropriate, however, to give parents samples of the test that are not in the public domain.

Students

Many of you have had students ask, "How did I do on the test?" As stated earlier in the chapter, students have the right to see their assessment results, but it's helpful for them to have you explain how they are progressing. Again, you don't want to discourage students, but you also need to be honest so that they can monitor their own learning. One way to help students monitor their learning is to host student-led conferences.

Student-Led Conferences

Who can tell the story of their learning progress better than the students themselves? Students rarely have the opportunity to share their perspectives about their learning, but student-led conferences is one way to help them take more responsibility for doing so.

In student-led conferences, you, the parent(s) or guardian(s), and the student meet to discuss the student's progress. Typically, you would meet with the student several weeks in advance and discuss test results, graded papers, and works in progress. Then you would guide the student to select three or four of their assessments to share at the conference. You can develop guidelines that fit your students' needs. For example, if you have state test information, you can require that the results are one of the assessments that students must share. After students have selected a few examples of their work, they should develop a list of their strengths, areas for improvement, and goals. For example, if Tanya achieved the "nearly met" benchmark on the state reading test, and she also shared a piece of scored writing and a free reading book list, she might say that she is aware that she needs to have better reading comprehension and that she is expanding her reading list to include more challenging books to help her improve. At this time in the conference, Tanya can ask you or her parents for additional guidance. As the teacher, you can give suggestions at the conference and also take notes on the conference to assist Tanya on ways to achieve her goals. The bottom line is that Tanya is presenting her achievements and taking responsibility for her continual progress.

As you can see from this example, you will not be merely defending a grade you have given or explaining assessments, you'll be part of a team, which includes the student, in strategizing about ways to help the student learn. To keep the conversation on track, you might want to develop an agenda for the conference, perhaps have the student present his or her work and goals for the first 5 minutes, and then give parents time to respond. At that point, you could add your own observations to round out the story. You might also want to end with specific goals for the student, the parents, and yourself.

If you're thinking that student-led conferences would be too difficult to implement, start small. Perhaps you could have students select and explain one piece of work and have them be part of a traditional conference for 5 minutes. You can experiment with what works for you and your students.

CHAPTER 9

The Assessment Story

Learning from the Past, Looking to the Future

In 2016, the National Council of Teachers of English (NCTE) released a study based on a survey called the Assessment Story Project. The survey of 530 educators around the United States showed that teachers are assessment literate, but they find that many mandated assessments are not meaningful. Respondents identified several alternatives to those assessments that they viewed as not contributing to their stories or the stories of their students. These included "embedded" assessments, presentations to other stakeholders (e.g., administrators, parents), and other forms of measurement.

We concur with the findings and recommendations in the Assessment Story Project (NCTE, 2016). The survey offered two recommendations that emphasized the importance of trusting teacher expertise in designing and using informative assessment practices, both formative and summative. The report concludes that teachers offer perspectives because of their expertise that are not available to policymakers and test creators.

We believe that, too often, high-stakes assessments are focused on the needs of policymakers and legislators and not as much on the students themselves. We hope that this book has been helpful to you as you learn about or review assessment literacies. Schooling may be the only institution that touches all of our lives every day. At some point, we all went to school or participated in schooling. We may have children or grandchildren in school. If you are reading this book, you probably work in a school. The benefits to society of schooling are well documented. Perhaps because so many lives are affected by the schools in our communities, so many want and should have a voice in how schools are operated. However, the voice most suited to expert assessment is the voice of the teacher.

Teachers can and should look for opportunities to inform assessment policy. Advocating for effective assessment that highlights what students can do, what kinds of problems they can solve, and what innovations they can create is an important role for us as educators. Advocacy includes being conversant about assessment in our communications with policymakers, parents, administrators, and especially our students. Advocacy also means guiding our students to being able to tell their own stories. Student-led parent conferences, portfolios and the new "electronic backpacks," peer review, and co-constructed rubrics are all places to start.

Assessment practices and tools have strengths and limitations, so when we recognize what they are, we are better able to construct the story our assessments can tell with precision. Not all superheroes wear capes. Many superheroes, the heroes of this book, are teachers, and their superpower is shining the light on what their students can do and have achieved.

BIG DATA TELL A STORY

Where might literacy assessment go from here? We asked our friends at Data Monsters (*https://datamonsters.com*) in Palo Alto and Moscow to give us a tour of educational technologies that might be used for assessment purposes, including feedback. In our final boxed feature, we learn how "big data" and artificial intelligence (AI) technologies inform and change assessment for teaching and learning. We finish our tour with what big data and AI technologies might make possible in the near future for education.

STORIES FROM RESEARCH

Data Monsters is a research and development lab and consulting company based in Palo Alto, California. It provides professional services with artificial intelligence (AI) and real-time big data. In this story, Olga Davydova and Dmitry Malkov outline the current and future applications of AI and big data to student assessment.

Big Data and Artificial Intelligence Capabilities in Students' Progress Assessment

OLGA DAVYDOVA AND DMITRY MALKOV

Each day schools and other educational organizations generate a huge amount of data of different types and formats. These data are indicators of learning processes, student assessments, varied surveys and reports, and information collected from school cameras, microphones, motion detectors, and so on. The data could be structured (stored in databases or spreadsheets in a format easily queried, read, and analyzed by a computer), unstructured (not contained in a classical row-column database but include text or multimedia), or semistructured (not organized into a database, but include semantic tags or metadata that makes their processing easier). The Programme for International Student Assessment (PISA) evaluates education systems worldwide by testing science, mathematics, reading, collaborative problem solving, and the financial literacy skills of 28 million students in 72 countries and contains a huge amount of structured data, or charts consisting of responses from individual students, school principals, and parents.[1] The amount of information nowadays is measured in terabytes (1,024 gigabytes), petabytes (1,024 terabytes), exabytes (1,024 petabytes), and even zettabytes (1,024 exabytes). These extremely large and usually unstructured datasets that cannot be processed or analyzed by a conventional computer are called "big data." Big data are now widely used and have greatly transformed the retail, financial, consumer technology, health care, and telecommunications sectors, as well as other industries.

What role does big data have in education? Big data may have a significant impact on education and student performance, depending on how it is used. It can make schools more effective and personalized, helping students learn on a higher level. Big data not only let educators track students' progress but also are able to determine their challenge points, show what and how improvements should be done, and develop better curriculums, teaching methods, and learning modes. Big data can support teachers in their daily work, helping them to communicate with students more effectively and assess their work and give them feedback faster in real time. Big data also let teachers better manage their own time.

AI also plays an important role in education. AI is a computer science field that studies and creates intelligent machines that act like humans. AI has already been applied in many areas, including information retrieval, speech recognition, face recognition, computer vision, fraud detection, monitoring and diagnosis, natural language processing, machine translation, chatbots and intelligent agents' development, virtual reality, and so on. AI can be a significant part of modern learning environments and makes possible the development of customizable learning interfaces or even digital games that suit students of any age group and level. Online lectures and video conferences are becoming a convenient way to teach and study. Cram101, MasteryConnect, Canvas, and Google Classroom are examples of applications built on AI. To facilitate the teaching process, Cram101 converts standard textbooks into a more visual and digestible format that contains chapter summaries, practice quizzes, and flashcards.[2] Using MasteryConnect software, teachers are able to send tests to their students via mobile devices, to scan and score paper assignments, to effectively assess core standards, to monitor student performance, and to report student achievements to parents

---

[1] *www.oecd.org/pisa/aboutpisa.*

[2] *http://cram101.com/facts101/wwwroot/hm.asp?c=&d=&a=&b=&u=.*

and administrators.[3] With the help of Canvas, a learning management system, teachers may use audio and video to communicate with students and give them instructions, assessments, and feedback online.[4] Google Classroom lets teachers create classes, distribute assignments, and send feedback in one place.[5]

All students are different and have their own personalities and learning preferences. Some pupils are visual learners, others are hands-on. For some students, it's better to watch; for others, to read or practice. Some students learn fast, others at a slower pace. Some students like to solve problems step-by-step; others solve problems in a nonlinear manner. The same lesson can be too easy for one student and too hard or boring for another one. Big data using students' profiles (data and observations) are able to classify students into different groups and even offer strategies and instructional content for the individual student. In the Method Schools in California, students are assembled every day into several groups based on their previous assessments and some personal information and work on specific areas of study.[6] The outcomes are dependent on how much students learn.

What indicators are usually measured? To create a student profile that can be used for a personalized education approach, many different types of data should be collected based on long-term surveillance. Not only are learning indicators important, but personal experiences and behaviors also play a major role. Martin Lindstrom, Danish author and *Time* magazine Influential 100 Honoree, called it "small data" in his book *Small Data: The Tiny Clues That Uncover Huge Trends*.[7] Data about students' behaviors in the classroom, how students interact with teachers and fellow students, emotional states and engagement level, attention span, disciplinary issues, language and vocabulary use, economic situation and social habits, and demographic, health, and home environment details are collected and leveraged.

AltSchool, a series of micro-schools that focus on personalized learning in San Francisco and New York, widely uses facial recognition algorithms and computer-vision technologies.[8] By analyzing facial expressions, individual keystrokes or mouse clicks, gestures, the movements of students' eyes on a computer screen, how well the student kept his or her attention, and so on, it is easy to determine how effective and interesting the lesson or certain activity is.

Students' speech can be converted to a text with help of text-to-speech and voice recognition tools like Amazon Lex[9] and then added to a data collection.

---

[3] *www.masteryconnect.com/features.html.*

[4] *www.canvaslms.com.*

[5] *https://classroom.google.com.*

[6] *www.methodschools.org/about-us-beta.*

[7] *www.martinlindstrom.com/our-books/small-data.*

[8] *www.altschool.com.*

[9] *https://aws.amazon.com/lex.*

Another very important type of data is data directly related to the learning process. Here are some examples: the student's prior knowledge, grade level, academic performance, attendance, favorite subjects, and individual interests; how quickly the student masters key concepts; which activities the student spent the most time on and which were ignored; the time spent on assignments and exams; and the number of assessments completed. All homework, quizzes, grades, test scores, self-assessments, international student assessments, reports, and surveys are also collected. Even parent call logs are gathered. Using these data, teachers can find ways to improve teaching techniques and students' performance

In the past, the curricula consisted of certain fixed learning plans for all students, in spite of the fact that students had different backgrounds and levels of academic performance. The assignments and the grading process were well tested and not complicated, but not always effective. Big data can change this situation by offering the best approach and unique personalized teaching for each student. The so-called "adaptive learning" or "personalized learning" educational computer-based method modifies the form of material presentation according to student's knowledge, specific needs, performance, pace, interests, and preferences. AI lets teachers identify individual students' challenge points, customize learning plans and assignments, and recommend the best ways of learning new material. Many digital tools have been created to provide adaptive learning technology. The MagicBox, an interactive learning platform, uses big data to identify gifted students and offer advanced materials and more challenging problems to them.[10] DIBELS reading assignments are applied at Roosevelt Elementary School near San Francisco to identify students who need help with their weak spots.[11] Moodle is another free online learning platform developed for teachers, administrators, and students to create personalized learning environments.[12] Adaptive learning lets the student stay motivated, decrease the time needed to learn new concepts, and improve learning outcomes.

Many schools still use standardized tests to determine if the student understands a subject, and teachers still spend too much time grading regular assignments. A low test score automatically meant that the student did not master the material. However, many people started to question this kind of test as an imperfect way to assess a student's knowledge. Big data offer many different student-grading techniques in real time that are more reliable, convenient, and effective. The more advanced systems are able, for example, to change test items, depending on how students perform on earlier questions. Almost all the assignments can be reviewed automatically with excellent precision. Big data not only allow evaluators to determine students' mistakes and problem areas in knowledge but also boost learning transparency and let administrators evaluate trends in education.

[10] *www.getmagicbox.com.*

[11] *https://dibels.uoregon.edu.*

[12] *https://moodle.org.*

education. A computer system can even instruct the student about where to find detailed information on misunderstood concepts. After finishing the test, all the information is gathered and it is immediately available to both the teachers and students. The student can get personalized feedback and help from the teacher fast. The student can see not only his or her answers on an assessment, but can compare the results with those of his or her classmates. Teachers and administrators are able to view students' performance at the individual or collective levels. An advantage is that students can be widely tested and data reviewed independently. Student self-assessment techniques also can be applied.

AI can also help teachers to identify copied text in academic papers or make sure that the students' work is original. Turnitin is a cloud-based educational tool that detects plagiarism, performs content verifications, and evaluates written work.[13]

When viewing student's grades, teachers can grade themselves by obtaining information on how well students mastered various concepts. If the results are not good, the teachers should consider adjustments in their lesson plans.

Another useful feature of big data is information sharing at a school, country, or even worldwide level. For example, when the teacher meets a new student, all the data about the student's performance, challenges, and strong spots in lessons and assignments can be visualized in an efficient way.

All the student assessments are often stored in tables or spreadsheets. These formats are convenient for analysis but not very readable for most people. To help teachers and administrators easily understand and visualize this information, special color-coded dashboards with a simple user interface were developed. They are easy to use and do not require any expertise. For example, Michigan State incorporated a dashboard that shows the different indicators for student outcomes in such dynamics as improving, staying the same, or declining in different areas.[14] Usually, the real-time information can be explored at a whole-school or individual-student level. The system shows students' performances, achievements, and issues in general or by a specific subject. In addition, the dashboards indicate students who need more challenging tasks, require help, or are at risk of dropping out, letting the teachers change their lesson plans accordingly. If needed, informative and well-formatted reports can be created and exported to different file formats. Parents can also get access to the dashboards.

The DreamBox dashboards give administrators and teachers easy access to real-time student activity, proficiency data, and trends to more effectively personalize learning.[15]

In the first International Conference on Learning Analytics and Knowledge that took place in Banff, Alberta, in 2011, "learning analytics" was determined

---

[13] *www.turnitin.com/solutions/plagiarism-prevention.*

[14] *www.michigan.gov/midashboard.*

[15] *www.dreambox.com.*

as the measurement, collection, analysis, and reporting of data about learners and their contexts, for purposes of understanding and optimizing learning and the environments in which it occurs.[16] In the Gartner's Supply Chain Executive Conference in 2013, four types of analytics were denoted, including descriptive analytics, diagnostic analytics, predictive analytics, and prescriptive analytics.[17] Descriptive analytics is oriented to the past and determines what has happened, whereas diagnostic analytics tries to understand the reasons why a particular event happened. Predictive analytics builds statistical models that help to figure out what can happen. Prescriptive analytics can give advice on what should be done to get the best possible outcomes. This scheme works in education very well. After the data are collected, it is important to discover the positive and negative trends and patterns they reveal. By comparing previous data and patterns with a student's current data, it is possible to predict where he or she will struggle in school or his or her state standardized test scores. Predictive analytics can identify the students who are able to complete more demanding assignments or who have specific issues and the students who are likely to fail a class or who risk dropping out unless they receive extra help. Outliers (a measurement that is distant from other measurements) sometimes can lead to very surprising conclusions.

Project U-Turn in Philadelphia, for example, uses big data and analytics to identify the reasons for high dropout rates and seeks ways to decrease it.[18] The Spokane Public Schools district in Washington uses an early warning system that compares individual students with past dropouts' records and predicts future high school dropouts while students are still in elementary school and time to take action to prevent dropping out.[19] Arizona State University uses Knewton's Adaptive Learning Platform, data-driven software that analyzes students' keystrokes and mouse clicks.[20] By taking into account students' grades, learning performances, strengths and weaknesses, and even hesitation patterns when using the computer mouse, the software is able to give recommendations to teachers about the students who need individual help. Predictive analytics also finds the flaws in the curricula, letting teachers optimize teaching techniques and styles for individual students, tailor their educational program, and finally stop to make decisions based on their intuition. At the same time, analytics allow for evaluating the impact of new pedagogical approaches. The key is to safely use reliable and accurate data and know how to interpret them correctly, not forgetting that big data reveal a correlation, not causation, among the data collected.

Like Amazon, which uses recommendations as a marketing tool, or Best Buy, which applies a recommendation system to increase revenue, educational

---

[16] https://tekri.athabascau.ca/analytics.

[17] https://blogs.gartner.com/matthew-davis/top-10-moments-from-gartners-supply-chain-executive-conference.

[18] www.projectuturn.net.

[19] www.spokaneschools.org/Domain/3445.

[20] www.knewton.com.

institutions can also embed recommendation systems. AI is able to offer learning paths for students and recommend methodologies in study materials. Some applications are able to match students with appropriate teachers. Using big data, teachers can suggest subjects and classes to students that they might like and determine the jobs that suit them the best, taking into consideration job-market predicted needs.

Using big data, special knowledge bases for teachers could be created. These knowledge bases can contain information on the best teaching techniques and curriculums, different types of assignments for students, and modes for their assessment. The main features of such knowledge bases should be quick access to needed information and the ability to ask and answer questions and to communicate effectively with colleagues.

Appendices

APPENDIX A

Assessing the Assessments: Gathering Information and Evidence

Assessing the Tools

This instrument is designed to analyze and evaluate the different assessment tools used by teachers in class. This assessment serves teachers in terms of "assessment for learning" since it can help them measure the effectiveness of their assessment techniques used throughout the year with their students. Accordingly, they can modify, amend, or change their applied assessment techniques to be able to assess their students more effectively. This is a general assessment tool that is also designed to be applied in many contexts, including different grade levels, different class subjects, different educational systems, and so forth. The criteria in this tool are derived from the assessment steps that teachers originally go through with their students in any educational cycle.

Assessment for Learning Checklist

Standards:

Objectives:

Date:

Class:

Subject:

Teacher:

Observer:

(continued)

From *Assessment Literacy: An Educator's Guide to Understanding Assessment, K–12,* by Thomas DeVere Wolsey, Susan Lenski, and Dana L. Grisham. Copyright © 2020 The Guilford Press. Permission to photocopy this appendix is granted to purchasers of this book for personal use or use with students (see copyright page for details). Purchasers can download enlarged versions of this appendix (see box at the end of the table of contents).

Assessing the Assessments: Gathering Information and Evidence *(page 2 of 3)*

(C) Content (P) Process (Pr) Product	Assessment Tool	Gathering Information and Evidence						
	Description	Questioning	Observation	Quizzes, Tests, and Exams; Other Work Products	Checklists	Rubrics	Self-Assessment	Peer Assessment
Student Work Products or Activity	**Description**	Teacher asks focused and planned questions to ensure understanding of the material.	Teacher systematically observes and monitors students, including checking for understanding.	Teacher collects written evidence of what the students have learned.	Teacher measures students' learning by matching it to specific criteria in relation to learning outcomes.	Teacher effectively communicates expectations of quality and grading at different levels of achievement.	Teacher allows students to reflect on their own performance, supplying them with defined criteria to measure against.	Teacher allows students to reflect on the performance of their colleagues, supplying them with defined criteria to measure against.
Homework and Assignments	Teacher assigns students with relevant homework and assignments that further enforce understanding.							
Informal and Quick Checks Checking for Understanding	Teacher uses exit slips, minute paper, polling with technology.							

(continued)

Assessing the Assessments: Gathering Information and Evidence *(page 3 of 3)*

Presentations	Teacher allows students to show their learning of the material by presenting it to their classmates.			
Projects	Teacher allows students to deepen and show connection in their learning by working on individual/group projects.			
Behaviors and Dispositions	Teacher promotes behaviors such as collaboration, on-task work, classroom routines, cognitive strategies, and critical thinking.			
Comments				

Assessing the Assessments: Interpreting and Analyzing Assessment Data

Assessment Checklist: Interpreting

Date:

Class:

Subject:

Teacher:

Observer:

Standards:

Student Learning Objective(s)	Type or Format of Assessment Source	Supporting Information
☐ Students will be able to identify and analyze the claims made in a written argument. ☐ Students will select and construct claims for an argument essay they will write.	☐ Questioning ☐ Discussion ☐ Quick assessment (e.g., exit slip) ☐ Written product ☐ Performance ☐ Observation ☐ Portfolio ☐ Other	☐ Rubric ☐ Checklist ☐ Scoring guide ☐ Models and exemplars ☐ Directions oral or written ☐ Other student materials (texts, computer, etc.)
Artifact or Performance represents ☐ Content ☐ Process ☐ Product	Information obtained	Planned feedback
Teacher effectively measures student learning in relation to learning objectives.	How do you know?	

(continued)

From *Assessment Literacy: An Educator's Guide to Understanding Assessment, K–12*, by Thomas DeVere Wolsey, Susan Lenski, and Dana L. Grisham. Copyright © 2020 The Guilford Press. Permission to photocopy this appendix is granted to purchasers of this book for personal use or use with students (see copyright page for details). Purchasers can download enlarged versions of this appendix (see box at the end of the table of contents).

Student Learning Objective(s)	Type or Format of Assessment Source	Supporting Information
Teacher effectively measures student performance in relation to his/her performance at a prior time—Baseline assessment or data.	How do you know?	
Learning tasks and performances are appropriately complex relative to standards.	How do you know?	
Learning tasks provide appropriate challenge and guidance with visible progress indicators.	How do you know?	
☐ Student ownership of learning evident. • Self-assessment • Peer assessment	What evidence of ownership is available?	

171

Assessing the Assessments: Quality

Date:

Class:

Subject:

Teacher:

Observer:

Standards and Objectives:

Assessment Quality

	1–5 Scale	Notes
Reliability	Teacher's assessment methods would provide consistent results if performed by other teachers, if learning is measured using various methods, or if student learning is measured at different times.	
Comments		

(continued)

From *Assessment Literacy: An Educator's Guide to Understanding Assessment, K–12,* by Thomas DeVere Wolsey, Susan Lenski, and Dana L. Grisham. Copyright © 2020 The Guilford Press. Permission to photocopy this appendix is granted to purchasers of this book for personal use or use with students (see copyright page for details). Purchasers can download enlarged versions of this appendix (see box at the end of the table of contents).

Assessing the Assessments: Quality *(page 2 of 2)*

		1–5 Scale	Notes
Validity	Teacher's assessment methods accurately and precisely measure student learning with respect to the intended learning and the targeted learning outcomes.		
Comments			

Reference Points

			Notes
	Teacher effectively measures student learning in relation to learning outcomes.		
	Teacher effectively identifies student performance in relation to other students.		
	Teacher effectively measures student performance in relation to his or her performance at a prior time.		
Comments			

173

Assessing the Assessments: Documenting and Record Keeping

Date:

Class:

Subject:

Teacher:

Observer:

Standards and Objectives:

Documenting and Record Keeping			
Student Records	Teacher keeps detailed records of observations of student learning over time.		
Student Portfolios	Teacher keeps a collection of student work that reflects accomplishments and growth.		
Comments			

(continued)

174

From *Assessment Literacy: An Educator's Guide to Understanding Assessment, K–12*, by Thomas DeVere Wolsey, Susan Lenski, and Dana L. Grisham. Copyright © 2020 The Guilford Press. Permission to photocopy this appendix is granted to purchasers of this book for personal use or use with students (see copyright page for details). Purchasers can download enlarged versions of this appendix (see box at the end of the table of contents).

	Reporting and Feedback			
Report Cards	Teacher prepares periodic summaries of student learning for parents.			
Teacher–Student Conferences	Teacher meets periodically with students to provide detailed feedback and direction to guide student learning.			
Teacher–Parent Conferences	Teacher meets periodically with parents to discuss the students' learning and plan next steps.			
Feedback	What feedback has been provided, and what actions taken to enact feedback?			
Comments				

Cumulative Feedback Table

Title of the Paper/Genre:	
Teacher's Comments and Questions about Paper 2:	**Student's Comments and Questions:**
Grade or rubric subgrades can go here:	

(continued)

Used by permission of Arlene R. H. Pincus.

From *Assessment Literacy: An Educator's Guide to Understanding Assessment, K–12,* by Thomas DeVere Wolsey, Susan Lenski, and Dana L. Grisham. Copyright © 2020 The Guilford Press. Permission to photocopy this appendix is granted to purchasers of this book for personal use or use with students (see copyright page for details). Purchasers can download enlarged versions of this appendix (see box at the end of the table of contents).

Assignments (each number is a new assignment):	1	2	3	4	5	6	7	8	9
Purpose and audience:									
Is my lead compelling?									
Did I tell the reader what the reader needs to know?									
Does my ending work?									
Strong writing: (examples below)									
Descriptions: specific adjectives (examples: a *sizzling* meal, a *compelling* question)									
Strong Verbs: powerful verbs (examples: ? and ?)									
And so on . . . (lines can be added or deleted)									
Revising:									
Order of ideas. (example: student considers whether the information is given in a user-friendly order)									
Consider whether all of the ideas belong in this paper.									
And so on . . . (lines can be added or deleted)									
Editing:									
Please **use the spelling and grammar checker.**									
Check for run-on sentences (highlighted in green). Copy two of the three run-on sentences below and show how you would like to edit each.									

References

Adams, M. J. (2011). Advancing our students' language and literacy: The challenge of complex texts. *American Educator, 34*(4), 3–11, 53.

Afflerbach, P. (2007). *Understanding and using reading assessment, K–12.* Newark, DE: International Reading Association.

Afflerbach, P. (2018). *Understanding and using reading assessment, K–12* (3rd ed.). Alexandra, VA: ASCD.

Afflerbach, P., Pearson, P. D., & Paris, S. G. (2008). Clarifying differences between reading skills and reading strategies. *The Reading Teacher, 61*, 364–373.

Ainsworth, L. (2015). *Common formative assessments 2.0: How teacher teams intentionally align standards, instruction, and assessment.* Thousand Oaks, CA: Corwin Press.

Allington, R. L. (2002). You can't learn much from books you can't read. *Educational Leadership, 60*(3), 16–19.

Anderson, L. W., & Krathwohl, D. R. (Eds). (2001). *A taxonomy for learning, teaching, and assessing: Revision of Bloom's taxonomy of educational objectives.* New York: Longman.

Andrews, M., Brown, R., & Mesher, L. (2018). Engaging students with assessment and feedback: Improving assessment for learning with students as partners. *Practitioner Research in Higher Education Journal, 11*(1), 32–46.

Argyris, C., & Schon, D. A. (1996). *Organizational learning: II. Theory, method, and practice.* Reading, MA: Addison-Wesley.

Atwell, N. (1987). *In the middle: Writing, reading, and learning with adolescents.* Portsmouth, NH: Heinemann.

Bang, M. (1988). *The paper crane.* Hong Kong: South China Printing.

Betts, E. A. (1946). *Foundations of reading instruction, with emphasis on differentiated guidance.* New York: American.

Black, P., & Wiliam, D. (1998, October). Inside the black box: Raising standards through classroom assessment. *Phi Delta Kappan, 80*(2), 139–144, 146–148.

Black, P., & Wiliam, D. (2009). Developing the theory of formative assessment. *Educational Assessment, Evaluation and Accountability, 21*(1), 5–31.

Bolman, L. G., & Deal, T. E. (2008). *Reframing organizations: Artistry, choice, and leadership* (4th ed.). San Francisco: Jossey-Bass.

Boud, D., & Molloy, E. K. (2013). Rethinking models of feedback for learning: The challenge of design. *Assessment and Evaluation in Higher Education, 38*(6), 698–712.

Bransford, J. D., Brown. A. L., & Cocking, R. R. (Eds.). (2000). *How people learn: Brain, mind, experience, and school.* Washington, DC: National Academies Press.

Broad, B. (2003). *What we really value: Beyond rubrics in teaching and assessing writing.* Logan: Utah State University Press.

Buckingham, M., & Goodall, A. (2019, March/April). The feedback fallacy. *Harvard Business Review* [Online]. Retrieved from *https://hbr.org/2019/03/the-feedback-fallacy.*

Burke, J. (2015). Teaching by design: Tools and techniques to improve instruction. *Journal of Adolescent and Adult Literacy, 59*(3), 249–260.

Burns, M. (2017). *#FormativeTech.* Thousand Oaks, CA: Corwin Press.

California Department of Education. (2018). California High School Exit Exam (CAHSEE). Retrieved from *www.cde.ca.gov/ta/tg/hs.*

CAST. (2011). *Universal Design for Learning Guidelines version 2.0.* Wakefield, MA: Author. Retrieved from *www.udlcenter.org/aboutudl/udlguidelines/principle1.*

Cennamo, K., Ross, J., & Ertmer, P. (2009). *Technology integration for meaningful classroom use.* Mason, OH: Cengage Learning.

Cohen, E. G. (1994). *Designing groupwork: Strategies for the heterogeneous classroom* (2nd ed.). New York: Teachers College Press.

Covey, S. (1989). *The seven habits of highly effective people.* New York: Simon & Schuster.

Cox, K., & Guthrie, J. T. (2001). Motivational and cognitive contributions to children's amount of reading. *Contemporary Educational Psychology, 26,* 116–131.

Creswell, J. W. (2005). *Educational research: Planning, conducting, and evaluating quantitative and qualitative research* (2nd ed.). Upper Saddle River, NJ: Prentice-Hall.

Culham, R. (2003). *6+1 Traits of Writing: The complete guide.* New York: Scholastic.

Cunningham, A. E., & Stanovich, K. E. (1998). What reading does for the mind. *American Educator, 22*(1/2), 8–15.

Cunningham, A., & Stanovich, K. (2003). Reading can make you smarter. *Principal, 83,* 34–39.

Curtis, C. P. (2004). *Bud, not Buddy.* New York: Dell.

Daines, D. (1986). Are teachers asking higher level questions? *Education, 106,* 368–374.

Dale, E., & O'Rourke, J. (1981). *The living word vocabulary.* Chicago: World Book–Childcraft International.

Docan-Morgan, T. (2015). The participation log: Assessing students' classroom participation. *Assessment Update, 27*(2) 6–7.

Dufflemeyer, F. A. (1994). Effective anticipation guide statements for learning from expository prose. *Journal of Reading, 37,* 452–457.

Durkin, D. (1981). Reading comprehension instruction in five basal reader series. *Reading Research Quarterly, 16*(4), 515–544.

Durkin, D. (1990). Dolores Durkin speaks on instruction. *The Reading Teacher, 43*(7), 472–726.

Dyer, K. (2017). Understanding formative, interim, and summative assessment and their role in student learning. Retrieved from *www.nwea.org/blog/2017/understanding-formative-interim-summative-assessments-role-student-learning.*

Ehri, L. C. (1994). Development of the ability to read words: Update. In R. Ruddell, M. Ruddell, & H. Singer (Eds.), *Theoretical models and processes of reading* (4th ed., pp. 323–358). Newark, DE: International Reading Association.

El Koumy, A. (2009). Effect of classroom performance assessment on EFL students' basic and inferential reading skills [Report]. Retrieved December 16, 2018, from *https://files.eric.ed.gov/fulltext/ED514530.pdf.*

Emig, J. (1971). *The composing processes of twelfth graders*. Urbana, IL: National Council of Teachers of English.

Ferguson, H. (2013). Journey into ungrading. *Counterpoints, 451*, 194–209.

Fisher, D., & Frey, N. (2014). *Checking for understanding* (2nd ed.). Alexandria, VA: ASCD.

Fisher, D., Frey, N., & Hattie, J. (2016). *Visible learning for literacy, grades K–12: Implementing the practices that work best to accelerate student learning*. Thousand Oaks, CA: Corwin Press.

Fluckiger, J. (2010). *Single point rubric: A tool for responsible student self-assessment* (Paper 5). Omaha: Teacher Education Faculty Publications, University of Nebraska. Retrieved April 25, 2014, from *http://digitalcommons.unomaha.edu/tedfacpub/5*.

Fonseca, J., Carvalho, C., Conboy, J., Valente, M., Gama, A., Salema, M., & Fiúza, E. (2015). Changing teachers' feedback practices: A workshop challenge. *Australian Journal of Teacher Education, 40*(8), 59–82.

Freire, P. (1993). *Pedagogy of the oppressed*. New York: Continuum. (Original work published 1970)

Frey, N., & Fisher, D. (2013). A formative assessment system for writing improvement. *The English Journal, 103*(1), 66–71.

Fullan, M., Hill, P., & Crévola, C. (2006). *Breakthrough*. Thousand Oaks, CA: Corwin Press.

Freire, P. (1993). *Pedagogy of the oppressed: 30th anniversary edition*. New York: Continuum.

Gambrell, L. B. (2011). Seven rules of engagement: What's most important to know about motivation to read. *The Reading Teacher, 65*(3), 172–178.

Gardiner, S. (2001). Ten minutes a day for silent reading. *Educational Leadership, 59*(2), 32–35.

Gay, G. (2010). *Culturally responsive teaching* (2nd ed.). New York: Teachers College Press.

Gick, M. L., & Holyoak, K. J. (1983). Schema induction and analogical transfer. *Cognitive Psychology, 15*, 1–38.

Goodman, Y. (1985). Kid watching: Observing children in the classroom. In A. Jaggar & M. T. Smith-Burke (Eds.), *Observing the language learner* (pp. 9–18). Newark, DE: International Reading Association & National Council of Teachers of English.

Goodrich, H. (1997). Understanding rubrics. *Educational Leadership, 54*(4), 14–17.

Gottheiner, D. M., & Siegel, M. A. (2012). Experienced middle school science teachers' assessment literacy: Investigating knowledge of students' conceptions in genetics and ways to shape instruction. *Journal of Science Teacher Education, 23*(5), 531–557.

Graham, H. T., & Bennett, R. (1998). *Human resources management*. Harlow, UK: Pearson Professional.

Graham, S., & Perin, D. (2007). A meta-analysis of writing instruction for adolescent students. *Journal of Educational Psychology, 99*(3), 445–476.

Grisham, D. L., Lapp, D., Wolsey, T. D., & Vaca, J. (2014). Combining print and visual information via ePosters: Generating and displaying learning. *Journal of School Connections, 5*(1), 59–75.

Grisham, D. L., & Wolsey, T. D. (2005). Improving writing: Comparing the responses of eighth graders, preservice teachers and experienced teachers. *Reading and Writing Quarterly, 21*(4), 315–330.

Gronlund, N. E., & Linn, R. L. (1990). *Measurement and evaluation in teaching*. New York: Macmillan.

Guthrie, J. T., & Klauda, S. L. (2016). Engagement and motivational processes in reading. In P. Afflerbach (Ed.), *Handbook of individual differences in reading* (pp. 41–54). New York: Routledge.

Hattie, J. (2009). *Visible learning: A synthesis of over 800 meta-analyses relating to achievement*. New York: Routledge.

Hattie, J., & Timperley, H. (2007). The power of feedback. *Review of Educational Research, 77*(1), 81–112.

Hagstrom, F. (2006). Formative learning and assessment. *Communication Disorders Quarterly, 28*(1), 24–36.

Hemingway, E. (1952). *The old man and the sea.* London: Jonathan Cape.

Heritage, M. (2011, Spring). Formative assessment: An enabler of learning. *Better: Evidence-based Education Magazine.* Retrieved December 1, 2018, from *www.csai-online.org/sites/default/files/resources/4666/FA_Enabler_of_Learning.pdf.*

Hernandez, R. D. (1994). Reducing bias in the assessment of culturally and linguistically diverse populations. *Journal of Educational Issues of Language Minority Students, 14,* 269–300.

Hersey, P., Blanchard, K. H., & Johnson, D. E. (2001). *Management of organizational behavior: Leading human resources* (8th ed.). Upper Saddle River, NJ: Prentice-Hall.

Hiebert, E. H. (2018, March 16). Text complexity systems: A teacher's toolkit. *Text Matters—A Magazine for Teachers.* Retrieved from *http://textproject.org/library/text-matters/text-complexity-systems-a-teachers-toolkit.*

Hiebert, E. H., Goodwin, A. P., & Cervetti, G. N. (2018). Core vocabulary: Its morphological content and presence in exemplar texts. *Reading Research Quarterly, 53*(1), 29–49.

Hiebert, E. H., & Reutzel, D. R. (2010). *Revisiting silent reading: New directions for teachers and researchers.* Newark, DE: International Reading Association.

Howell, C. A. (2013). *Development and analysis of a measurement scale for teacher assessment literacy.* Unpublished master's thesis, Department of School Psychology, Eastern Carolina University, Greenville, NC.

Hunter, M. (1982). *Mastery teaching.* Thousand Oaks, CA: Corwin Press.

Huot, B., & Neal, M. (2006). Writing assessment: A techno-history. In C. A. MacArthur, S. Graham, & J. Fitzgerald (Eds.), *Handbook of writing research* (pp. 417–432). New York: Guilford Press.

Hyland, K. (1990). Providing productive feedback. *ELT Journal, 44*(4), 279–285.

Iyengar, S. S., & Lepper, M. R. (2000). When choice is demotivating: Can one desire too much of a good thing? *Journal of Personality and Social Psychology, 79,* 995–1006.

Jackson, C. W., & Larkin, M. J. (2002). Teaching students to use grading rubrics. *Teaching Exceptional Children, 35*(1), 40–45.

Johnston, P. (2004). *Choice words: How our language affects children's learning.* Portsmouth, NH: Stenhouse.

Jones, F. (2007). *Tools for teaching* (2nd ed.). Santa Cruz, CA: Fredric H. Jones & Associates.

Karim, K., & Nassaji, H. (2018). The revision and transfer effects of direct and indirect comprehensive corrective feedback on ESL students' writing. *Language Teaching Research.* [Epub ahead of print]

Karkouti, I., Wolsey, T. D., & Toprak, M. (2019). *Syrian refugees in Lebanese schools: Social support.* Manuscript in progress.

Keil, F., interviewed by Moosath, A. (2015, July). Ripple effect. *Indian Management.* Retrieved from *https://krw-intl.com/wp-content/uploads/2015/08/Coverage-22nd-July-2015-Return-on-Character_-IMA.pdf.*

Khatri, S. (2012). The kafala system strikes again. Retrieved from *http://dohanews.co/post/3945711534/the-kafala-system-strikes-again.*

Kim, K. H., & Zabelina, D. (2015). Cultural bias in assessment: Can creativity help? *International Journal of Critical Pedagogy, 6*(2), 129–148.

Koedinger, K., Booth, J., & Klahr, D. (2013). Education research: Instructional complexity and the science to constrain it. *Science, 342,* 935–937.

Kohn, A. (1993, October). The case against gold stars. Retrieved from *www.alfiekohn.org/article/case-gold-stars-2.*

Korzybski, A. (1933). *Science and sanity: An introduction to non-Aristotelian systems and general semantics.* Englewood, NJ: International Non-Aristotelian Library/Institute of General Semantics.

Kronheim, J. M. (1875). Five little pigs. Retrieved from *https://americanliterature.com/author/joseph-martin-kronheim/short-story/five-little-pigs.*

Ladson-Billings, G. (2006). From the achievement gap to the education debt: Understanding achievement in U.S. schools. *Educational Researcher, 35*(7), 3–12.

Ladson-Billings, G. (2013). Lack of achievement or loss of opportunity? In P. L. Carter & K. G. Welner (Eds.), *Closing the opportunity gap: What America must do to give every child an even chance* (pp. 11–22). New York: Oxford University Press.

Lapp, D., Wolsey, T. D., & Wood, K. (2014). *Mining complex texts: Using and creating graphic organizers to grasp content and share new understandings 6–12.* Thousand Oaks, CA: Corwin Press.

Lemov, D., Woolway, E., & Yezzi, K. (2012). *Practice perfect: 42 rules for getting better at getting better.* San Francisco: Jossey-Bass.

Leu, D. J., Forzani, E., Rhoads, C., Maykel, C., Kennedy, C., & Timbrell, N. (2015). The new literacies of online research and comprehension: Rethinking the reading achievement gap. *Reading Research Quarterly, 50*(1), 1–23.

Leu, D. J., Kulikowich, J., Sedransk, N., Coiro, J., Forzani, E., Maykel, C., & Kennedy, C. (2014, April 4). *The ORCA Project: Designing technology-based assessments for online research, comprehension, and communication.* Philadelphia: American Educational Research Association.

Levinson, A., Russo, A., & Russo, I. (Producers), & Hiller, A. (Director). (1984). *Teachers* [Motion picture]. United States: United Artists.

Manitoba Education, Citizenship, & Youth. (2006). *Rethinking classroom assessment with purpose in mind: Assessment for learning, assessment as learning, assessment of learning.* Winnipeg, ON, Canada: Author.

Manning, M., Lewis, M., & Lewis M. (2010). Sustained silent reading: An update of the research. In E. H. Hiebert & D. R. Reutzel (Eds.), *Revisiting silent reading: New directions for teachers and researchers* (pp. 112–128). Newark, DE: International Reading Association.

McCarthy, J. (2014). 3 guidelines to eliminating assessment fog. *Edutopia.* Retrieved from *www.edutopia.org/blog/differentiated-instruction-eliminating-assessment-fog-john-mccarthy.*

McCormack, R. L., & Pasquarelli, S. L. (2010). *Teaching reading: Strategies and resources for grades K–6.* New York: Guilford Press.

McGregor, D. (1960). *The human side of enterprise.* New York: McGraw-Hill.

Meier, D. (2000, February/March). Educating a democracy: Standards and the future of public education. *The Boston Review, 24*(6). Retrieved from *http://bostonreview.net/archives/BR24.6/meier.html.*

MetaMetrics. (2019). What is a Lexile® measure? Retrieved from *http://lexile.com/about-lexile/lexile-overview.*

Milner, H. R., IV. (2015). *Start where you are, but don't stay there.* Cambridge, MA: Harvard Education Press.

Montague, J. (2013). Desert heat: World Cup hosts Qatar face scrutiny over "slavery" accusations. Retrieved from *http://edition.cnn.com/2013/04/30/sport/football/football-qatar-world-cup-2022-worker-rights/index.html.*

Montgomery, K. (2000). Classroom rubrics: Systematizing what teachers do naturally. *The Clearing House: A Journal of Educational Strategies, Issues and Ideas, 73*(6), 324–328.

Moser, G. P., & Morrison, T. G. (1998). Increasing students' achievement and interest in reading. *Reading Horizons: A Journal of Literacy and Language Arts, 38*(4), 233–245.

Mueller, C. M., & Dweck, C. S. (1998). Praise for intelligence can undermine children's motivation and performance. *Journal of Personality and Social Psychology, 75*(1), 33–52.

National Council of Teachers of English Assessment Task Force. (2016). The Assessment Story

Project. Retrieved from *www2.ncte.org/research/research-summaries/assessment-story-project/report*.

National Governors Association Center for Best Practices & Council of Chief State School Officers (NGA & CCSSO). (2010). *Common Core Standards for English language arts and literacy in history/social studies, science, and technical subjects.* Washington, DC: Authors.

National Institute for Child Health and Human Development. (2000). *Report of the National Reading Panel: Teaching children to read* (NIH Pub. No. 00-4769). Washington, DC: National Institutes of Health. Retrieved from *www.nichd.nih.gov/publications/pubs/nrp/smallbook*.

National Research Council. (2001). *Knowing what students know: The science and design of educational assessment.* Washington, DC: National Academies Press.

National University. (2010). Student teaching handbook. Retrieved from *www.nu.edu/assets/resources/departmentResources/Student%20Teacher%20Handbook%202010%20Final.pdf*.

NGSS Lead States. (2013). *Next Generation Science Standards: For states, By states.* Washington, DC: National Academies Press.

Northwest Regional Educational Laboratory. (2001). 6+1 Trait® writing. Retrieved from *http://educationnorthwest.org/traits*.

O'Connor, K. (2018). *How to grade for learning: Linking grades to standards* (4th ed.). Thousand Oaks, CA: SAGE.

Organisation for Economic Co-operation and Development. (2011). *Students on line: Reading and using digital information.* Paris: Author. Retrieved from *http://dx.doi.org/10.1787/9789264112995-en*.

Palincsar, A. S., & Brown. A. L. (1984). Reciprocal teaching of comprehension-fostering and comprehension-monitoring activities. *Cognition & Instruction, 1*, 117–175.

Panadero, E., & Jonsson, A. (2013). The use of scoring rubrics for formative assessment purposes revisited: A review. *Educational Research Review, 9*, 129–144.

Partnership for Assessment of Readiness for College & Careers. (2017). Assessments: Next generation assessments. Retrieved from *https://parcc-assessment.org/assessments*.

Pashler, H., McDaniel, M., Rohrer, D., & Bjork, R. (2008). Learning styles: Concepts and evidence. *Psychological Science in the Public Interest, 9*(3), 105–119.

Paulk, W. (2001). The Cornell note-taking system [adaptation]. Retrieved from *http://lsc.cornell.edu/notes.html*.

Paulsen, G. (1987). *Hatchet.* New York: Trumpet Club/Scholastic.

Pearson, P. D., & Gallagher, M. (1983). The instruction of reading comprehension. *Contemporary Educational Psychology, 8*(3), 317–344.

Pentimonti, J. M., & Justice, L. M. (2010). Teachers' use of scaffolding strategies during read alouds in the preschool classroom. *Early Childhood Education Journal, 37*(4), 241–248.

Peters, T. J., & Waterman, R. H. (2004). *In search of excellence: Lessons from America's best-run companies.* New York: HarperCollins.

Popham, W. J. (2009). Assessment literacy for teachers: Faddish or fundamental? *Theory Into Practice, 48*(1), 4–11.

RAND Study Group. (2002). *Reading for understanding: Toward an R&D program in reading comprehension.* Arlington, VA: Author. Retrieved from *www.rand.org/pubs/monograph_reports/2005/MR1465.pdf*.

Ramaprasad, A. (1983). On the definition of feedback. *Behavioral Science, 28*(1), 4–13.

Rattan, A., Good, C., & Dweck, C. S. (2012). "It's Ok—Not everyone can be good at math": Instructors with an entity theory comfort (and demotivate) students. *Journal of Experimental Social Psychology, 48*(3), 731–737.

Renninger, K. A., & Bachrach, J. E. (2015). Studying triggers for interest and engagement using observational methods. *Educational Psychologist, 50*(1), 58–69.

Reutzel, D. R., & Fawson, P. C. (2002). *Your classroom library: New ways to give it more teaching power.* New York: Scholastic Professional Books.

Rosenblatt, L. (1995). *Literature as exploration* (5th ed.). New York: Modern Language Association of America.

Ross, G., & Spielberg, A. (Producers), & Marshall, P. (Director). (1988). *Big* [Motion picture]. United States: 20th Century Fox.

Rowlands, K. D. (2007). Check it out!: Using checklists to support student learning. *The English Journal, 96*(6), 61–66.

Sadler, D. R. (2013). Opening up feedback: Teaching learners to see. In M. Yorke & S. Merry (Eds.), *Reconceptualising feedback in higher education: Developing dialogue with students* (pp. 54–63). Abingdon, UK: Routledge.

Saltelli, A., & Funtowicz, S. (2014, Winter). When all models are wrong. *Issues in Science and Technology, 30*(2). Retrieved from *https://issues.org/andrea.*

Schlemmer, L. (2019, March 26). New "backpack" program has JCPS students show what they learned—without a test [89.3 WFPL News, Louisville, KY]. Retrieved from *https://wfpl.org/new-backpack-program-has-jcps-students-show-what-they-learned-without-a-test.*

Schunk, D., & Mullen, C. (2009). Self-efficacy as an engaged learner. In K. R. Wenzel & A. Wigfield (Eds.), *Handbook of motivation at school* (pp. 237–291). New York: Routledge.

Scott, V. (2013). Moving guide: 10 things to know before moving to Qatar. Retrieved from *www.telegraph.co.uk/expat/before-you-go/10053737/Moving-guide-10-things-to-know-before-relocating-to-Qatar.html.*

Seker, H., & Kömür, S. (2008). The relationship between critical thinking skills and in-class questioning behaviours of English language teaching students. *European Journal of Teacher Education, 31*(4), 389–402.

Serdyukov, P., & Ryan, M. (2008). *Writing effective lesson plans: The 5-star approach.* Boston: Pearson.

Spiro, R. J., Feltovich, P. J., & Coulson, R. L. (1996). Two epistemic world-views: Prefigurative schemas and learning in complex domains. *Applied Cognitive Psychology, 10,* 51–61.

Springer, S. E., Harris, S., & Dole, J. A. (2017). From surviving to thriving: Four research-based principles to build students' reading interest. *The Reading Teacher, 71*(1), 43–50.

Stiggins, R. (2005). *Student-involved assessment for learning* (4th ed.). Upper Saddle River, NJ: Pearson, Merrill, Prentice Hall.

Stockman, A. (2015) Three moves learners should make visible [Blog post]. Retrieved from *www.angelastockman.com/blog/2015/05/26/three-moves-learners-should-make-visible.*

Strachan, S. L. (2015). Kindergarten students' social studies and content literacy learning from interactive read-alouds. *Journal of Social Studies Research, 39*(4), 207–223.

Taylor, B. M., Frye, B. J., & Maruyama, G. M. (1990). Time spent reading and reading growth. *American Educational Research Journal, 27*(2), 351–362.

Tomlinson, C. A., & Moon, T. R. (2013). *Assessment and student success in a differentiated classroom.* Alexandria, VA: ASCD.

Truby, J. (2007). *The anatomy of a story.* New York: Farrar, Straus & Giroux.

Vandevoort, L., Amrein-Beardsley, A., & Berliner, D. (2004). National board certified teachers and their students' achievement. *Education Policy Analysis Archives, 12*(46), 1–45.

Vitto, J. (2003). *Relationship-driven classroom management.* Thousand Oaks, CA: Corwin Press.

Vygotsky, L. S. (1978). *Mind in society: The development of higher psychological processes* (M. Cole, V. John-Steiner, S. Scribner, & S. Souberman, Eds.). Cambridge, MA: Harvard University Press. (Original work published 1934)

Wasserstein, R. (2010). George Box: A model statistician. *Significance, 7,* 134–135.

Watson, J. D., & Crick, F. H. C. (1953). A structure for deoxyribose nucleic acid. *Nature, 171,*

737–738. Retrieved from *www.nature.com/scitable/content/Molecular-Structure-of-Nucleic-Acids-16331.*

Welner, K. G., & Carter, P. L. (2013). Achievement gaps arise from opportunity gaps. In P. L. Carter & K. G. Welner (Eds.), *Closing the opportunity gap: What America must do to give every child an even chance* (pp. 1–10). New York: Oxford University Press.

Wigfield, A., & Guthrie, J. T. (1997). Relations of children's motivation for reading to the amount and breadth of their reading. *Journal of Educational Psychology, 89*(3), 420–432.

Wiggins, G. (2012). Seven keys to effective feedback. *Educational Leadership, 70*(1). Retrieved from *www.ascd.org/publications/educational-leadership/sept12/vol70/num01/Seven-Keys-to-Effective-Feedback.aspx.*

Wiggins, G., & McTighe, J. (2005). *Understanding by design* (expanded 2nd ed.). Alexandria, VA: ASCD.

Wiliam, D. (2011). What is assessment for learning? *Studies in Educational Evaluation, 37*(1), 3–14.

Wilson, M. (2006). *Rethinking rubrics in writing assessment.* Portsmouth, NH: Heinemann.

Wilson, M. (2007/2008). The view from somewhere. *Educational Leadership, 65*(4), 76–80.

Wirth, K., & Perkins, D. (2005). Knowledge surveys: An indispensable course design and assessment tool (Innovations in the Scholarship of Teaching and Learning). Retrieved from *http://serc.carleton.edu/files/garnet/knowledge_surveys_indispensabl_1313423391.pdf.*

Wiseman, A. (2011). Interactive read alouds: Teachers and students constructing knowledge and literacy together. *Early Childhood Education Journal, 38*(6), 431–438.

Wolsey, T. D. (2006). Exploring the territory: Teachers as cartographers. *Journal of Adolescent and Adult Literacy, 49,* 460–465.

Wolsey, T. D. (2008). Efficacy of instructor feedback in an online graduate program. *International Journal on eLearning, 7*(2), 311–329.

Wolsey, T. D. (2014). Accuracy in digital writing environments: Read up, ask around, double-check. *Voices from the Middle, 21*(3), 49–53.

Wolsey, T. D. (in press). Secondary transitions—Egypt. *Bloomsbury Education and Childhood Studies.*

Wolsey, T. D., Grisham, D. L., & Hiebert, E. (2012). What is text complexity?: Module 1. Retrieved from *http://textproject.org/library/professional-development/teacher-development-series.*

Wolsey, T. D., & Lapp, D. (2017). *Literacy in the disciplines: A teacher's guide for grades 5–12.* New York: Guilford Press.

Wolsey, T. D., Lapp, D., & Dow, B. (2010). Reading practices in elementary schools: Format of tasks teachers assign. *Journal of Research in Innovative Teaching, 3,* 101–112.

Yasso, T. J. (2005). Whose culture has capital?: A critical race theory discussion of community cultural wealth. *Race Ethnicity and Education, 8*(1), 69–91.

Young, J. R., Scales, R. Q., Grisham, D. L., Dobler, E., Wolsey, T. D., Smetana, L., . . . Yoder, K. K. (2017). Student teachers' preparation in literacy: Cooking in someone else's kitchen. *Teacher Education Quarterly, 44*(4), 74–97.

Zenger, J., & Folkman, J. (2014, January 15). Your employees want the negative feedback you hate to give [Blog post]. *Harvard Business Review.* Retrieved from *https://hbr.org/2014/01/your-employees-want-the-negative-feedback-you-hate-to-give.*

Zenger, J., & Folkman, J. (2016). Feedback—the powerful paradox [White paper]. Retrieved from *https://zengerfolkman.com/wp-content/uploads/2013/03/ZF-Feedback-The-Powerful-Paradox.pdf.*

Index

Note. *f* or *t* following a page number indicates a figure or a table.